D1287210

ISBN 0-900-157-19-4

British Library Cataloguing in Publication Data.

A catalogue record for this book is available from the British Library.

CROSS PURPOSES

Shock and Contemplation in Images of the Crucifixion

Curated by Nathaniel Hepburn

MASCALLS GALLERY, Paddock Wood, Kent — 5 March – 29 May 2010

BEN URI, The London Jewish Museum of Art — 15 June – 19 September 2010

FOREWORD

Richard Harries (Lord Harries of Pentregarth) is Gresham Professor of Divinity and an Honorary Professor of Theology at King's College, London. He is the author of *Art and the Beauty of God*, Mowbray 1993, *The Passion in Art*, Ashgate, 2004, and "Jesus in Art", in *Jesus in History, Thought, and Culture, An Encyclopedia*, ed. Leslie Houlden, ABC-CLIO, 2003.

For much of Christian history there has been a close association between forms of Platonism and the Christian faith. This has meant that God has been thought of as sublime beauty, as well as perfect goodness and absolute truth. So St Augustine quite naturally addresses God as "O thou beauty most ancient and withal so fresh." But if the marks of beauty are wholeness, harmony and radiance, as Aquinas thought, how can art depict the bleakness and suffering of life? Either the beauty of the art will be so consoling it will cheapen the reality of the suffering: or the hurt and ugliness will be so stark that there will seem little wholeness, harmony or radiance in the work.

This dilemma was particularly acute in the 20th century, often termed the worst in human history. The carnage of World War I, Soviet purges and above all the Holocaust led artists to stress the harshness of life. This was reinforced by "the masters of suspicion", above all Freud, who left all harmonizing features in both religion and art open to question. "All that consoles is fake" as Iris Murdoch put it.

These dilemmas come into sharpest focus in depictions of the cross. For crucifixion was one of the cruelest forms of torture devised by cruel human beings. Yet Christian artists have turned Christ's cross into great works of art. How can we stand before a depiction of the crucifixion other than appalled? Particularly if we stand there in Christian faith seeing a symbol of what day by day we inflict on both God and one another? Yet the urge to go on depicting the cross in works of art continues, from both those who share the Christian faith and those who don't. These are just some of the deep questions raised by the powerful works in this exhibition, some of which are addressed by Ben Quash in his essay in this catalogue.

I believe the organisers of this exhibition are to be highly congratulated. Reading this catalogue I found myself totally absorbed by the range and quality of the paintings chosen, and by the equally well chosen commentators upon them. Many of the works are very little known to a wider public and they deserve to be. It is particularly good to have the *Apocalypse en Lilas, Capriccio* by Chagall, together with the opportunity to look at Chagall's windows in All Saints' Tudeley. Given the history of oppression of Jews by Christians, with the cross often being viewed with fear as a symbol of this oppression, it is remarkable that Chagall chose to symbolise the anguish of his fellow Jews through a suffering Jesus, not only in his famous *White Crucifixion* but in a number of other works as well. This is one of the most remarkable exhibition of paintings on a religious theme for many years and it deserves to be widely recognised as such.

CURATOR'S INTRODUCTION: NATHANIEL HEPBURN, MASCALLS GALLERY

Art and religion are, for me, very closely linked; that spiritual feeling found in a church, a mosque or a synagogue is the same feeling I get in front of a beautiful painting. Art, like religion, also enables us to address areas beyond our understanding: death, life, pain, fear, love. Marc Chagall's stained glass windows adorning All Saints' Church in Tudeley is a perfect example of an artistic expression of love which creates an atmosphere of calm and contemplation.

Although Modernism brought with it many changes, 20th century artists continued to address grand biblical and mythological themes albeit often re-presented within contemporary contexts. In *Cross Purposes* we explore one specific symbol – the Crucifixion – and how Christ's death has been re-told and re-employed as a symbol to command attention by artists over the last hundred years.

The stimulus for *Cross Purposes* was Chagall's stained glass windows of All Saints' Church in Tudeley, just three miles away from Mascalls Gallery, and the opportunity to contrast the narrative of the Crucifixion in his East window with other depictions of this theme. Within *Cross Purposes* you will be able to compare Eric Gill's carved wooden crucifixion, Graham Sutherland's harrowing scene inspired by Holocaust photographs, John Armstrong's dynamic painting and many others including Chagall's very private representation *Apocalypse en Lilas, Capriccio* from 1945.

Enormous appreciation to Patricia Dunkin Wedd from Tudeley Church for the inspiration to bring the Chagall drawings for All Saints' Church to the UK for the first time and thanks to Centre Pompidou in Paris for agreeing to loan them. We are delighted to be sharing this exhibition with Ben Uri Gallery, The London Jewish Museum of Art. It is a fine organisation with a long history with which we are proud to be associated. It is remarkable fortune that David Glasser, Chair of Ben Uri, discovered a previously unknown Chagall crucifixion painting and brought it to the UK for the Museum and the nation. It is a very important addition to *Cross Purposes*.

This exhibition has been the work of many people but our thanks must first go to the lenders and artists who have agreed to have the works shown in Cross Purposes. Their support and encouragement have been a constant source of energy. I thank Helen Robertson for designing the catalogue and all those who have contributed. It is a rare privilege to have such a breadth of distinguished commentators agree to produce new work on the subject and it has been an equally rare delight to share long discussions with many about the works. My particular thanks to Jennifer Swan who generously shared her insight into all the works and helped me to shape the exhibition concept.

A huge amount of work on this exhibition has been contributed by the team of Interns at Mascalls Gallery including Aaron Tebano, Joanne Tweddle, Helen Copsey, Jennifer Price and Laura Bryars and I thank them all. *Cross Purposes* at Mascalls Gallery would not have been possible without the generous support of Prof and Mrs Hans Rausing, The Jerusalem Trust, the Christian Arts Trust, NADFAS Tonbridge, and the many people who attended fundraising concerts at All Saints' Tudeley. This engaging catalogue would not have been possible without The Dorset Foundation and the full partnership of Ben Uri, The London Jewish Museum of Art who present the exhibition in London from 15 June until 19 September 2010.

BEN URI: DAVID J GLASSER, CO CHAIR (EXECUTIVE)

Much revealing scholarship and commentary by eminent theologians, art historians, critics, and artists has been written for this catalogue addressing the Crucifixion from a wide range of standpoints.

We hope Cross Purposes will rekindle discussion as to whether the Crucifixion within an artistic context was and remains exclusively a Christian experience and solely a part of Christian iconography.

For centuries the Crucifixion was a principal motif in an artist's repertoire and was very much a Christian experience. One explanation revolves around the observance of the Commandment 'Thou shalt not have any graven image' deterring and forbidding within Judaism (and Islam) the creation of any alternative image to the Almighty. In strictly orthodox Jewish (and no doubt Muslim) communities such observance still all but eliminates the option of art as a profession.

From the 16th to the 19th centuries, assimilation amongst European Jewry was not the norm. During this period it is often assumed Jewish artists distanced themselves from the Crucifixion as it was a taboo. The reality was that portraiture was the taboo hence the void of practising Jewish artists in any numbers until the late 19th century and thus the relative void of Jewish artists addressing the Crucifixion during that period.

However the opposite is true of the 20th century. The age of emancipation allowed Jewish artists to join and contribute to the most radical and creative century in the history of the visual arts. Within an atmosphere of change, which saw traditions dilute and Modernism change many agendas, the image of the Crucifixion has been transformed from the specific to the generic, which is illustrated perfectly through this exhibition.

The image of the Crucifixion in the 20th century has become a universal and accessible symbol – a shared experience, a shared heritage. Some Jewish artists including Chagall and Levy before and during the Second World War and Bak (a survivor) after used the Crucifixion to illustrate the persecution and then the slaughter of Jews, Gypsies and homosexuals by the Nazis. Shock and drama is hugely enhanced by these artists distancing themselves from traditional iconography to present a contemporary and Jewish Jesus on the Cross. Their message reflected the irony that Christ was a Jew (Y'shua being his biblical name) and now his followers were slaughtering his brethren and by association their own.

Questions will also no doubt be asked as to the appropriateness of Ben Uri, The London Jewish Museum of Art, partnering Mascalls Gallery in presenting Cross Purposes. Why then did Ben Uri embrace this challenging exhibition?

Ben Uri, founded in 1915 in Whitechapel in London's East End, is Britain's oldest Jewish cultural institution. It is a distinguished Jewish Museum of Art with a very distinctive dual heritage in both the Jewish community and the history of British and European 20th century art. Ben Uri is uniquely positioned representing the Jewish community in the heart of this country's mainstream arts arena.

The Museum's ethos 'The Art Museum for Everyone' reflects the art and experiences of the 300 or so artists represented in the collection. Exhibitions often juxtapose émigré artists (irrespective of religious backgrounds) fleeing from oppression in the beginning and middle of the 20th century with today's emerging masters who often know nothing less than complete freedom of expression. We survey and contrast their work and as importantly tell their stories.

Throughout the ages, when the visual arts were not an option, Jewish craftsmen contributed widely to Church art particularly in the area of ceremonial objects. To complement studies on this subject Ben Uri had for some years been planning an exhibition examining and comparing the use of Christian and Jewish iconography in modern and contemporary art. The opportunity to partner Cross Purposes and add a wider understanding and appreciation of the subject, its sensitivities and of the two religions matched our original vision perfectly.

Ben Uri partners and embraces this exhibition for its artistic merit, scholarship and stimulus for much discussion on each of the works shown and the artists' intentions.

ALL SAINTS' CHURCH, TUDELEY: PATRICIA DUNKIN WEDD, ART CO-ORDINATOR

The stained glass windows of All Saints' Tudeley are designed for worship and contemplation and the East window is a memorial. Chagall has surrounded the crucifixion of the East window with scenes which show God's creation – "all flocks and herds, and the beasts of the field, the birds of the air, and the fish of the sea" – as well as angels and the figures of Adam and Eve in the Garden of Eden. The Chief Rabbi, Lord Sacks, says "The concept that Art can add spirituality is something that goes to the core of all religions ... Marc Chagall's stained glass can but serve to enhance the spirituality of the beautiful surroundings in which they are placed, advance the fervour with which the Almighty is worshipped, and increase the devotion of those coming under the inspiration of Chagall's divinely-inspired talent."

Beyond the spiritual, Chagall's windows are works of art, and are some of the finest works of religious art in the country. All Saints' Tudeley is a place of cultural as well as religious pilgrimage and in 2007 we were approached by the Vitromusée Romont in Switzerland which was presenting an exhibition of Chagall's designs for his windows around the world. This is the first time we saw early designs for Tudeley's windows and the seed of an idea was planted to bring these drawings to the UK and show them in close proximity to the final works of art. We are delighted that Mascalls Gallery jumped at the idea!

Cross Purposes counterposes Tudeley's windows with other depictions of the crucifixion by artists of the 20th and 21st centuries creating a powerful and thoughtful exhibition. In the works, many emotions are at work, with Tudeley's benevolent Christ set against the loneliness of Maggi Hambling's 2002 *Good Friday* and the vital spontaneity of Tracey Emin's *The Disposition*; we see the alluring simplicity of Eric Gill and the bitter gall of Graham Sutherland.

ESSAYS

A CHRISTIAN CRUCIFIXION: IS THE CROSS A SYMBOL FOR UNIVERSAL HUMAN EXPERIENCE?

By Ben Quash

Ben Quash is the first Professor of Christianity and the Arts at King's College London. Until 2007 he was Dean and Fellow of Peterhouse in the University of Cambridge. He is a Canon Theologian of Coventry Cathedral and is developing new postgraduate courses on Faith and the Arts in collaboration with the National Gallery, London. His recent publications include *Theology and the Drama of History*, *Fields of Faith: Theology and Religions for the 21st Century*, and *Heresies and How to Avoid Them: Why It Matters What Christians Believe.*

The cross, for Christians, is central to all reality. It is the presence of God's covenant at the heart of the world, the covenant in whose strength the world was created in the first place. The entire world drama is concentrated on and hinges on the cross, for the cross guarantees the world's bond with its creator. The creation of the world, we might say, already had the cross written into it implicitly, as the assurance that God would stay with the world, and do whatever was required to maintain his fellowship with it. So Christianity can read backwards from the cross to God's everlasting covenant and from there to the original act of creation.

But the cross is not just a Christian symbol, and even amongst Christians it can be read in many ways. Some of this variety is present in *Cross Purposes*, and shows the cross's extraordinary fecundity as a provocative as well as a consoling image; political as well as devotional; subversive as well as iconic.

Some interpretations of the cross encourage us to see it as a paradigm of suffering-in-general. The implication here is that, if we have ever suffered, we can identify with and understand what the crucifixion means. And, it follows, we will be in a position to use images of the cross as *expressive* of our pain. Indeed, depicting the cross can serve as a prophetic gesture, intentionally drawing our attention to the injustices or cruelties perpetrated in our own day; calling attention to contemporary martyrdoms through the sign of the crucifixion. This was a part of Chagall's bold genius: to reclaim the cross as a symbol of *Jewish* suffering and martyrdom in the 20th century (as well as a symbol of the artist's own struggle). Other Jewish artists have since followed his example.

In a closely related move, the horror of the cross can be rendered a sort of 'sublime' moment, in which the almost unrepresentable aspects of its reality – those things that disrupt or dissolve all of our ordinary notions of form, beauty and proportion – are still (*just*) shown capable of figural rendering. It is perhaps no accident that the relatively modern 'rediscovery' of Matthias Grünewald's Isenheim altarpiece, with its tortured Christ figure, spoke so inspirationally to a swathe of 20th century artists trying to find an idiom that could do justice to the overwhelming disturbances of their epoch.

Although some works in this exhibition depict the cross as standing for all human suffering, one question these images raise is whether Christ's suffering on the cross is generalisable in that way. For it can surely be said that not all suffering is holy, and yet Christianity wants to say that Christ's particular suffering is. This seems to open another possible line of exploration of the significance of the cross for artists: an exploration not just of what is shareable in the cross on the basis of widespread human experience, but of what is emphatically unique, different, even glorious about it. For Christians, all human suffering may be within reach of the redemptive power of Christ's victory, which he won by dying as a man, but the cross was not a neat illustration of all and every kind of suffering. It was not a painful sickness or a sudden catastrophe, inexplicable and unpredictable. It was the end of a path freely chosen.

There is a strong current in Christian theology which says that Christ's death on the cross is an act of thanksgiving – we might say, an act of *eucharist*. Indeed the cross may be seen as the consummate act of thanksgiving: the eucharist of eucharists. It is not that Christ's suffering in human flesh should be of no importance for Christians, or unworthy of contemplation. It is rather that too much concentration on the crucifixion as *only* a moment of suffering entails the loss of other ancient and profound meanings of Christ's embrace of the cross – thoroughly trinitarian interpretations of the cross – many of which place the accent on thanksgiving. We might think of the words of that great hymn *Vexilla Regis*, which talks of the cross as a 'royal banner' making a triumphant progress through history. Or the ancient lines: 'by route of the cross, joy has come into the world'. If in the life of God the Trinity, the Father imparts to the Son all that is his ('all that is thine is mine,' as Jesus says in John 17:10), then the Son's outpouring is perhaps most truly understood as an *answer* to the gift of Godhead. It is a gift which is of truly equal substance to the Father's gift. In this return, we see a thanksgiving as selfless and unreserved as the Father's original self-impartation. The Son, like the Father, gives the best that he has to give. The Son, too, hands over all that he has received. The Son, too, spares nothing. The Son, too, declares to the Father how beloved he is to him. What this vision of divine love dares us to do is to see the cross as part of that joyous, abundant flow of the divine being which is already in God. The cross, in that sense, has a sort of godly *recklessness*; the Son makes a fitting response to the Father's total gift of himself by freely and thankfully allowing himself to be poured forth. As St. Thomas Aquinas says, it is not a question of God overpowering the suffering Son, but of a powerlessness in the Son which is the perfect expression of divine self-gift, and therefore 'because it is God's truth and righteousness, {a} powerlessness more powerful than all worldly power'.

This may be why depictions of Christ in the pre-Constantinian Church never showed him suffering. The cross of early Christian tradition was a glorious cross. The consciousness of his resurrection victory over the powers of sin and death was fresh and intense, and shaped what little specifically Christian art there was at all in a way that emphasised only new life, victory and the protection of the redeemed. There is none of that acute sense of his fleshly vulnerability, his agony and his death which was to be a feature of so much medieval, reformation and counter-reformation art. Later artists have from time to time repeated these sorts of emphases: Eric Gill, David Jones, Stanley Spencer, and Norman Adams among them.

Such artists help us to see how, from a Christian point of view, there is a structure to the world; a deep and sacrificial love that orders it. The structure is hinted at by the continual presence of what we might call 'cruciformity' in the Church's practices and in its art – like a sort of watermark through time. The cross discloses its pregnant form in each new stage of the human drama in the world. Perhaps the images in this exhibition show that process still underway; that watermark still discernible. These artists take their place in a tradition of imaging and re-imaging the cross, whose devotional importance for Christians signals something momentous: Christ's slow, patient movement through the ages, treading through the whole of human history, as the one in whom the world was created, by whose self-gift it is kept safe, and in whom it will find its destiny.

And for non-Christians? Well for those who do not believe this exhibition may have a different message, but one that is also of real importance. The cross is an enduring and profound part of Western artistic vocabulary, however secularised or late-modern we may think we have become. The point is well-made in an episode from Chaim Potok's novel *My Name is Asher Lev*. Asher Lev, Potok's protagonist (who is partly based on Chagall and partly on Potok himself), is a young Hasidic Jew with brilliant natural talent as a painter. However his strict religious upbringing sits in tension with this burgeoning creativity. At one point in the book Lev is taken to look at the crucifixion paintings at the Metropolitan Museum of Art by his mentor, a secular Jew called Jacob Kahn who himself paints and sculpts. Kahn wants Lev to learn from these pictures about 'the development of structure and form and expression, and the handling of pictorial space', but the images unsettle Lev and he asks to see no more of them. Kahn rounds on him:

"I am not telling you to paint crucifixions. *I am telling you that you must understand what a crucifixion is in art if you want to be a great artist. The crucifixion must be available to you as form.* Do you understand? No, I see you do not understand. In any case, we will see more crucifixions and more resurrections and more nativities and more Greek and Roman gods and more scenes of war and love – because that is the world of art, Asher Lev."

The crucifixion, is perhaps the image *par excellence* of Western art. 'To paint a crucifixion is to paint oneself into dialogue with all the great artists who have treated the theme in the past, from Masaccio to Picasso'[1]. As Kahn's comment suggests, by wrestling with the crucifixion 'as form' an artist struggles with his or her very place within art's unfolding story.

[1] See Aaron Rosen *Imagining Jewish Art: Encounters with the Masters in Chagall, Guston, and Kitaj* (Legenda Studies in Comparative Literature, 2009). I am indebted to Rosen for his use of the Potok quotation, which I follow him in using to make this point.

THE ARCHETYPAL NATURE OF CRUCIFIXION

By Jennifer Swan

Jennifer Swan is a psychologist and researcher in analytical theory and the arts. She has lectured in Fine Arts and humanities at universities in America and England, and is currently in private practice in the London area.

"Christ exemplifies the archetype of the self." C.G. Jung[1]

The crucifixion in art is linked to two millennia of Christianity, and most prominently as an image of religious ritual. *Cross Purposes* explores the crucifixion in art from the 20th and 21st centuries and the way that such works may function in a secular environment. The use of the crucifixion motif by artists in non-religious contexts supports arguments concerning the increasingly secularized relationship to organised religion. These works are viewed through their historical and personal content, where the image functions as a visual metaphor to establish or support the nature of an individual's suffering rather than providing a direct visual reference to organised religion.

In his work on the human psyche, the Swiss analyst Carl Jung studied the expression of symbols, focusing upon the relationship of symbols to individual and collective life experiences. Jung found evidence for his theory of the archetypes in interpreting commonly found images, particularly those that relate to Holy texts. Archetypes may be described as: "the inherited part of the psyche; structuring patterns of psychological performance linked to instinct; {and} a hypothetical entity irrepresentable in itself and evident only through its manifestations."[2] Archetypal theory remains debated in the analytical community, and theoretical points essential to this discussion are put forward with post-Jungian scholarship.

An archetype is detected through the manifestation of a symbolic expression, which often appears as an image in dreams or creative processes. These archetypal images are thought to emerge more frequently in periods of change, such as during times of war or religious reformation; though may also occur spontaneously as signifiers of individual growth. Jung theorised that examining and interpreting the presence of archetypal images revealed aspects of the individual psyche – e.g. the *ego* and *self* – and also provided evidence for an internal, psychic link to collective mankind.

The study of archetypes in relation to the structures of the human psyche forms the basis for an analytical approach to psychology. The psychic construct of the self is described as, "an archetypal urge to coordinate, relativise, and mediate the tension of the opposites[3]"[4] in our internal, psychic life. The self is universal, expansive, and transcends creed. In the form of an archetypal image, such as the Christ figure, the expression of self reveals "man's fullest potential and the unity of the personality as a whole."[5] For Jung, an analogy exists between the process of Christ's redemption – seen as a return to wholeness – and a psychic redemption, which may be viewed as the "integration of the collective unconscious which forms an essential part of the individuation process[6]."[7]

As an archetypal image, the crucified Christ engages both the individual and collective psyches. From an individual perspective, the artist is able to address his individuality in relation to an environment or experience, as related to an environment or experience. The artist may also be viewed as a conduit for the appearance of an archetype. The archetypal image is revealing for both the artist and audience through its capacity to connect with the psychic self. As a symbol, the crucifixion is universally recognisable; and within a secular context, it provides an engagement with each human being in a unique way irrespective of any faith.

The majority of the works in *Cross Purposes* were created independent of an organised religious commission, and present a secular context from which to discuss the emergence of an archetype through creative expression. The commissioned works of Chagall, Grant, Sutherland, and Stanley Spencer enrich the exhibition by providing a visual exchange between the secular and religious contexts. Through the creative process, the artists' relationship to an archetype intersects with the functional religious space. Visual themes in this exhibition are considered through the expression of the crucifixion motif in three instances: through an external, collective association, an internal, psychic reflection, and a spiritual or transcendent feature.

In the works of Sybil Andrews and Stanley Spencer, the crucifixion appears as part of an allegorical Biblical motif – the Golgotha mount. In this environment, multiple crosses and multiple figures suggest an external, physical engagement with the archetype. The allegorical appearance of the two thieves reflects the 'good' and 'evil' natures present in collective man and the internal, psychic tension inherent in their opposition. Jung observed that, "Whenever the archetype of the self predominates, the inevitable psychological consequence is a state of conflict vividly exemplified by the Christian symbol of crucifixion".[8] The archetypal manifestation through the multiple crosses emphasises presence and need for a reconciliation of opposing forces in order to achieve a state of psychic wholeness.

A second visual theme is represented in the group which includes the works of Roy de Maistre and Robert Henderson Blyth. These works present the artist's ability to address a sense of personal introspection through the creation of a symbol. In each of these crucifixions there exists a physicality, which is supported in the corporeal world, whilst reflecting an internal state of being. As such, it is not difficult to imagine that, for the artist, the convergence of both internal and external factors were relative in the process of creative expression through which an archetype of self is seen to emerge. As a viewer experiencing this singular, and often self-referential sense of the archetypal Christ, the numinous quality associated with archetypal expression becomes apparent.

A numinous quality is also evidenced in the third and final grouping, which includes the works of Craigie Aitchison, Maggi Hambling, and Norman Adams. These images support the analytical perspective of the artist as a conduit for the manifestation of an archetype through symbolic expression. This essence of the Christ figure is created through the visual transformation of the corporeal plane of reference, to encompass the sense of both spiritual, and psychic transcendence. The piece by Adams is of particular note in this grouping, as it incorporates a reference[9] to the psychic self through the symbol of the butterfly. This image appears integral with the archetypal Christ, and together, they reinforce and reflect the transformation process, and the transcendence associated with the emergence of the self.

The 'cross purposes' of the modern crucifixion theme are to be found in historic, cultural, and psychological perspectives. The modern depictions are an historical commentary, a metaphor of human identity and also a symbol of the transcendent, interior self. Examined here, it is a group of works unified through the emergence of an archetypal image, a concept valuable to an understanding of the way in which imagery is created and responded to by the individual and collective psyches. With the decline of the organised practice of faith in the 20th century, and the increasingly secularised view of personal spirituality, a contemporary psychic re-emergence of this historically Christian symbol is taking place. Underpinning the modern, secular expression of this archetypal image remains the essence of the transformative process, which presents a curious paradigm: a symbol of transformation, which is, itself, changing.

[1] Jung, C. (1959). *Christ, A Symbol of the Self.* In Aion: Researches Into the Phenomenology of the Self (R. Hull, Trans., Vol. 9ii, para. 70). Princeton, NJ: Princeton University Press.

[2] Samuels, A., Shorter, B., & Plaut, F. (1986). *A Critical Dictionary of Jungian Analysis.* London: Routledge & Kegan Paul, Ltd.

[3] The 'tension of the opposites' refers to a psychic impasse, where an individual's developmental progress is arrested and impeded. This impasse is resolved through transcendence; for the tension eventually produces a new, third possibility.

[4] Samuels, A., Shorter, B., & Plaut, F. (1986). *A Critical Dictionary of Jungian Analysis.* London: Routledge & Kegan Paul, Ltd.

[5] Ibid.

[6] The individuation process is, 'the key concept in Jung's contribution to the theories of personality development'. This process involves, '[a] person becoming himself, whole, indivisible, and distinct from other people or collective psychology.' Ibid.

[7] Jung, C. (1959). *Christ, A Symbol of the Self. In Aion: Researches Into the Phenomenology of the Self* (R. Hull, Trans., Vol. 9ii, para. 72). Princeton, NJ: Princeton University Press.

[8] Jung, C. (1959). *Christ, A Symbol of the Self. In Aion: Researches Into the Phenomenology of the Self* (R. Hull, Trans., Vol. 9ii, para. 125). Princeton, NJ: Princeton University Press.

[9] Stein, M. (2005). *Transformation: The Emergence of the Self* (2nd Edition ed.). College Station, TX: Texas A & M University Press.

THE CRUCIFIXION IN A HOLOCAUST CONTEXT

By Ziva Amishai-Maisels

Ziva Amishai-Maisels is Professor Emeritus in the Department of Art History at the Hebrew University of Jerusalem. She is the recipient of the Israel Prize for Art History, and the author of *Depiction and Interpretation: The Influence of the Holocaust on the Visual Arts*.

To many Jews and Christians the use of the Crucifixion to symbolize Holocaust victims is highly disturbing. Yet this usage stems from Christian and Jewish art and achieved legitimacy in the 1930s among members of both religions.

On the Christian side, the Passion had been used to express suffering in wars, either by suggestion – as in Francisco Goya's adoption of Christ's pose and stigmata for a victim in *The Third of May*, 1808 – or openly, as when George Grosz gave the Crucified boots and a gas mask to symbolize the soldiers killed in World War I[2]. This approach was adapted in the 1930s by German anti-Fascists to portray Christ as a victim of the Nazis. Thus in John Heartfield's *The Cross Was Not Heavy Enough* (1933), a Nazi soldier turns the cross Jesus carries on the way to Golgotha into a swastika[3]. In Otto Pankok's *The Passion* series (1933–34), Jesus is characterised as a Jew or a Gypsy, both of whom became Holocaust victims, and he is contrasted to his blond "Aryan" persecutors.[4] Pankok's message obviously struck a nerve as the Nazis forbade him to exhibit or to publish this series; they preferred to think of Jesus as an Aryan rather than a Jew. In rebuttal, Lutheran theologian Dietrich Bonhoeffer proclaimed that "an expulsion of Jews from the West must lead to an expulsion of Christ: because Jesus Christ was a Jew."[5] Some artists gave these words visual form: in England in 1941, John Amshewitz drew a Nazi priest storming from the pulpit: "All Jews must leave at once," whereupon Jesus gets down from his cross to go with them.[6]

Between 1933 and 1945, artists in other countries also utilised Christ to symbolize Fascist victims but usually did not stress that he was Jewish. This may be the case with Michael Rothenstein's *Crucifixion* of 1937 (p. 32), and it is clear in a sketch Renato Guttuso drew for his 1940 *Crucifixion*, where the soldier in the foreground assumes Hitler's face and rhetorical pose. Guttuso wrote in his diary: "I want to paint the passion of Christ as a scene of today...as a symbol for all those who suffered outrages, prison, torture, for their ideas."[7] The subject became so popular that a 1942 exhibition in New York highlighted works using the Passion to express the artists' personal reactions to events.[8] When such artists did suggest Christ's Judaism it was often not done overtly. In Oskar Kokoschka's *What are we fighting for?* (1943), the chest of the Crucified is branded "P.J." signifying "Perish Judea", a translation of the Nazi slogan "Juda verrecke". Kokoschka wanted to use the proceeds from this painting to help save Hungary's Jews.[9]

Many Jewish artists were more explicit about Jesus' Judaism, following a tradition that originated in Eastern European and German Jewish art in the 1870s. There the image of a Jewish Jesus was meant to convince Christians that contemporary anti-semitism and the pogroms it caused not only violated Christ's doctrines but were aimed against his brethren. The message was that those who killed Jews were crucifying Jesus anew.[10]

This approach is echoed in Marc Chagall's drawing of the Crucifixion seen through a window.[11] It was done in 1930 after a visit to Berlin convinced him of the Nazis' growing power, and in reaction to a pogrom on October 15, 1930, when the display windows of Jewish shops were smashed. To clarify his meaning, he replaced Jesus' loincloth with a Jewish prayer shawl with its distinctive stripes and tassels. In 1938, the Nazis' increasing persecution of the Jews led Chagall to use this image in a major work, *The White Crucifixion*.[12] Here Jesus' Jewish identity is indicated by his head-covering, the prayer shawl around his loins, the Aramaic inscription above his head and the menorah at his feet. Around him, as in a Russian icon, Chagall depicted explanatory scenes: pogroms, a synagogue burning on Crystal Night, and Jews fleeing in all directions from Nazi Germany, hinting at their lack of success in doing so through the boat stuck in a river on the left. In the picture's original state, inverted swastikas appeared on a Nazi flag above the burning synagogue ark and on the arm of the soldier before it, and a sign worn by a Jew on the left read "Ich bin Jude" (I am a Jew), recalling signs the Nazis utilised to humiliate Jews.[13] Although he later removed these overt symbols from the painting, its meaning remains clear.

While fleeing from France and after arriving in New York in 1941, Chagall used this symbolism to stress his identification with the suffering Jesus.[14] Although he continued to react to events, he cloaked them in general terms. Thus in *The Yellow Crucifixion* (1943), Jesus wears a prayer shawl as a loincloth and phylacteries, while his right arm lies under a Torah scroll to stress the Judeo-Christian tradition that had, however, not saved some 760 refugees on the *Struma* ship which is shown sinking on the left.[15] In *The Crucified* (1944), news of the destruction of Vitebsk caused him to paint orthodox Jews crucified in the streets of his birthplace.[16] In the *Apocalypse in Lilac: Capriccio* (p. 42), he reacted realistically to revelations about the gassing and mass shooting of Jews that became known after the liberation of the concentration camps. Since these Jews had been stripped naked before being killed, he not only depicted nude men and women being killed near a barbed wire fence at the bottom of the painting, but displayed a naked Jesus with a prayer shawl flowing down his back, and phylacteries on his head and arm. Jesus opens one eye to stare balefully at the Nazi before him, and uses his foot to block the Nazi's attempt to reach both the ladder of the Deposition and the Jewish victims beside it. Chagall also tried to render the Nazi powerless by chopping off his hand and stabbing his leg.[17]

Chagall was not the only Jewish artist to paint the Crucifixion of a modern Jew. In England, Emmanuel Levy – possibly inspired by Chagall's *White Crucifixion* – painted his own explicit *Crucifixion* that he dated 1942 (p. 34). Levy portrays a religious Jew in a prayer shawl and phylacteries being crucified under the word "Jude" (Jew), clearly referring to the reason Jews were being murdered in Nazi-occupied Europe. The cross is set in a Christian cemetery, against a background of ruins dominated by a church. This combination can be read in different ways. On the one hand, Jews are being killed by Christians and denied Jewish burial. On the other, the cemetery crosses and the ruins suggest that this murder has led to – and even symbolises – the destruction of Europe and its Christian culture. Josef Foshko's version of this theme, exhibited in New York in 1945, is even more aggressive. Here, an old Jew wearing a prayer shawl is crucified as he cries out: "Forgive them NOT, Father, for they KNOW what they do."[18]

This symbolism still occurs in Jewish art. Samuel Bak's *Study I* (1995, p. 62) is based on the photograph of the boy from the Warsaw ghetto who has become a symbol of the children who died in the Holocaust. Bak – who as a child in the Vilna ghetto had narrowly avoided being sent to his death – included several versions of this boy in his *Self-Portrait* of 1995–96 to symbolize his own friends who had not escaped the deadly transport and who still haunt him.[19] *Study I* interprets the boy's raised hands as being nailed to the cross, while the inverted triangle nailed to his chest is the negative of the badge worn by camp inmates. Unlike his frightened expression in the photograph, the boy here is worn out, and his head – framed by an open grate – is his only real part. His body is just suggested by the boards in front of him, and his hands, drawn on paper nailed to the cross' horizontal bar, are only a memory. He has not only been crucified but dismembered, a symbol of Holocaust victims who died in different ways.

After the Holocaust, the comparison between the Holocaust and the Passion became so common that when Dachau was liberated, its road was renamed "The Way of the Cross," and later Pope John Paul II called Auschwitz "the modern Golgotha."[20] Moreover, photographs of cruciform corpses discovered in the camps inspired artists such as Graham Sutherland, whose sketches for the *Crucifixion* for St. Matthew's Parish Church depict Jesus as bald and skeletal.[21] Whereas this source was played down in the altarpiece, it is clear in his 1947 *Crucifixion* (p. 46), with its more skeletal body, the hint of a bald pate under the crown of thorns, and the Y-shaped position of Christ's arms on the arched cross, details that duplicate those in the sketches. Although dead, Christ raises two fingers in a gesture of oration: he still has a message to communicate to mankind regarding their cruelty.

However, the post-Holocaust period also involved a crisis of faith in religion and humanity caused by the discovery of the depths of depravity to which the Nazis had sunk. This crisis of faith was rendered in Francis Bacon's variations on the Crucifixion, where man's bestiality triumphs and the Crucified has been turned into tortured meat.[22] Robert Henderson Blyth who had been with the British army when it invaded Germany and thus would have known of the cruciform corpses at Bergen Belsen, also created a hopeless situation in his *In the Image of Man* (1947, p. 44). Here, both crucified humanity and Christ are hollow, broken remnants of what they once were, and the ruins in the background, including the classical column, suggest that with the Holocaust and World War II, Western civilisation as it once was had perished. Even more despairing is one of Mathias Goeritz's crucifixion series ironically named *Redeemer of Auschwitz*, done in Mexico in 1951–53.[23] Here a charred Jesus, burnt in Auschwitz's ovens with his fellow Jews, reveals the destruction of the promised redemption for both the Jewish victims and the Christians who murdered them or stood idly by during the Holocaust.

[1] For more on this subject, see Ziva Amishai-Maisels, *Depiction and Interpretation: The Influence of the Holocaust on the Visual Arts* (Oxford, 1993), Part 2, Chapter 3: "The Crucified Jew".

[2] Ibid., fig. 114; Hans Hess, *George Grosz* (New Haven, 1985), p. 156. See also Richard Cork's comments on David Jones' *Crucifixion* below, p. 29.

[3] Wieland Herzfelde, John Heartfield, *Leben und Werk* (Dresden, 1971), pl. 158.

[4] Otto Pankok, *Die Passion* (Güttersloh, 1970).

[5] Erhard Frommhold, *Kunst im Widerstand* (Dresden, 1968), pp. 28–29.

[6] Sarah Briana Amshewitz, *The Paintings of J.H. Amshewitz* (London, 1951), pl. 89.

[7] Mario de Micheli, *Guttuso* (Milan, 1963), pl. 6, p. 69; Parma, Gallerie de Parma, Renato Guttuso (1963–64), p. 69.

[8] New York, Puma Gallery, *Modern Christs* (1942).

[9] D.J.R. Bruckner, Seymour Chwast and Steven Heller, *Art Against War* (New York, 1984), p. 94; Edith Hoffmann, *Kokoschka: Life and Work* (London, 1947), p. 237; J.P. Hodin, *Oskar Kokoschka: The Artist and his Time* (Greenwich, Conn., 1966), pp. 16–18.

[10] See Ziva Amishai-Maisels, "The Jewish Jesus," *Journal of Jewish Art 9* (1982), pp. 84–104.

[11] Amishai-Maisels, *Depiction and Interpretation*, fig. 393.

[12] See Ziva Amishai-Maisels, "Chagall's White Crucifixion," *Chicago Art Institute Bulletin 17* (no. 2, 1991), pp. 138–53.

[13] Cahiers d'art 14 (nos. 5–10, 1939), p. 152. He inverted swastikas to avoid depicting a hated symbol. See the deformed swastika in *Apocalypse in Lilac: Capriccio* (pl. xx).

[14] Amishai-Maisels, "Chagall's White Crucifixion," pp. 151–153; *Franz Meyer, Marc Chagall* (New York, 1963), catalogue no. 689.

[15] Amishai-Maisels, *Depiction and Interpretation*, colorplate 40.

[16] Ibid., fig. 390.

[17] See London, Ben Uri Museum and Osborne Samuel Gallery, *Apocalypse: Unveiling a lost masterpiece by Marc Chagall* (2010), pp. 5–16.

[18] New York, Ferragil Galleries, *Josef Foshko* (1945), cover.

[19] http://iconicphotos.files.wordpress.com/2009/10/stroop_report_-_warsaw_ghetto_uprising_06b.jpg&imgrefurl; *Lawrence Langer, Landscapes of Jewish Experience* (Boston, 1997), p. 37; Ziva Amishai-Maisels, "Haunting the Empty Place," in Stephen C. Feinstein, ed., *Absence/Presence: Critical Essays on the Artistic Memory of the Holocaust* (Syracuse, 2005), pp. 131–33.

[20] John M. Lenz, *Christ in Dachau* (Mödling bei Wien, 1960), p. 34; Berlin, Staatliche Museen, *Bilder vom Menschen in der Kunst des Aberlandes* (1980), p. 368. See the discussion in Amishai-Maisels, *Depiction and Interpretation*, pp. 187–88.

[21] Amishai-Maisels, *Depiction and Interpretation*, figs. 161, 166, 236, 400–401.

[22] Ibid., colorplates 44–45, 52.

[23] Amishai-Maisels, *Depiction and Interpretation*, pp. 196–97, fig. 411.

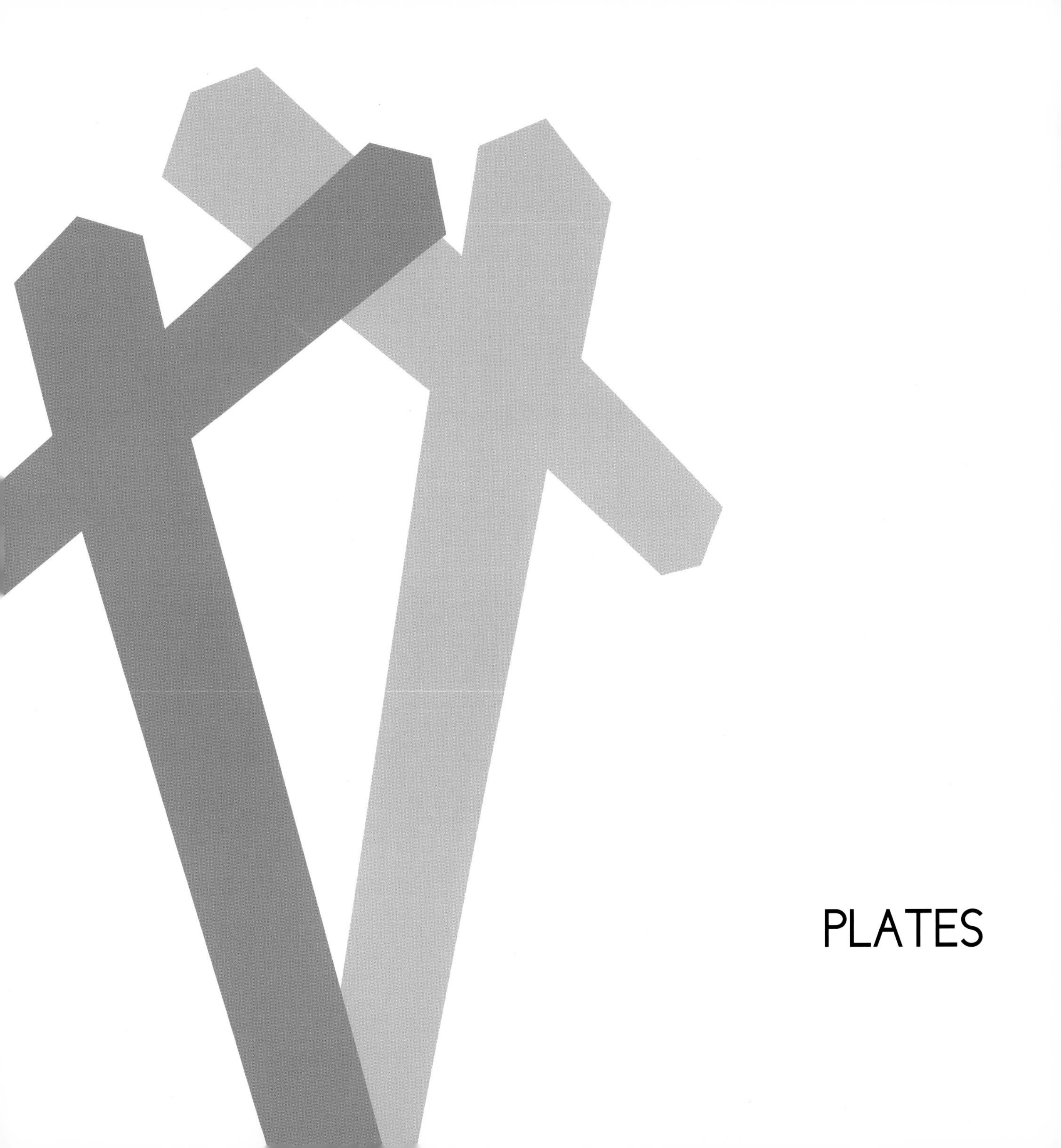

PLATES

I.N.R.I

GILBERT SPENCER (1892 – 1979)

THE CRUCIFIXION 1915

Frances Spalding is an art historian, critic and biographer and Professor of Art History at Newcastle University. Spalding is author of many books including *British Art since 1900* as well as biographies on the poet Stevie Smith, and the artists Roger Fry, Vanessa Bell, Duncan Grant, John Minton and Gwen Raverat. Her new book, *John Piper, Myfanwy Piper: Lives in Art* was published in September 2009.

This is a rare image of the Crucifixion: it focuses on the moment when the cross is being raised into position, with the result that the emphasis is as much on the labour involved as it is on Christ. The scene, therefore, is approached from a very human point of view. Moreover, it seems to be taking place not on Golgotha but more likely on the grassy area – Cookham Moor – which leads in to the village where Gilbert Spencer, the younger brother of the more famous Stanley Spencer, was born and brought up. These stocky, waistless lads, each with a shock of black hair, could be members of the Spencer family. It has even been suggested that the face of Christ, more patriarchal in appearance than is usual, bears a likeness to the artist's father. This is the man who used to read aloud the Bible stories to his children every night. They became a staple ingredient of their imaginative life. Stanley Spencer has put on record his childhood belief that, as he walked down the street, these holy scenes were taking place nearby, just the other side of the high garden walls. All his life he retained the belief that the everyday and the human are in close proximity.

Gilbert Spencer followed his brother to the Slade School of Art and, like him, had a striking independence and originality in his handling of imagery. What he did not have to quite the same extent was his brother's organisational wizardry in the handling of composition, nor the intensity of his vision. Nevertheless, once seen, this Crucifixion is impossible to forget. It is economically expressed: the white sky is already weighty with the approaching darkness that, in the Crucifixion narrative, covers the earth for three hours. And this contrast between light and dark is echoed in the clothing of the five young men pushing up the cross, as if to suggest that this event somehow implicates us all. They are stalwart figures, too, arms raised as they carry out their task, very much a significant part of the whole, but a part that few artists have had the imagination to conceive or portray. And the scene as a whole is held in tension by the diagonals pulling in opposite directions.

ERIC GILL (1882 – 1940)

CHRIST CRUCIFIED 1921

Ruth Cribb is at present working towards a PhD on Gill's sculpture at the University of Brighton and is working at the Victoria & Albert Museum. Ruth's exhibition *Eric Gill and Ditchling: The Workshop Tradition* was held at Ditchling Museum in 2007, and she also co-authored the accompanying book.

This wooden relief was carved to be the rood crucifix for the St Joseph and St Dominic Guild chapel in the village of Ditchling in Sussex, where Eric Gill had moved in 1907, and hung from the tie-beam in the chapel. Gill had converted to the Roman Catholic Church in 1913. Even before this, though, he was fascinated by the iconography of the Crucifixion. Gill established the Catholic art-workers Guild of St Joseph and St Dominic in 1921 with Hilary Pepler, Desmond Chute and Joseph Cribb.

Eric Gill initially trained as a draughtsman in an architect's office in London. He learnt stone masonry and calligraphy at evening classes, and subsequently set up his own business as a letter cutter. His many contacts in the London art world and Arts and Crafts movement enabled Gill to establish himself as a professional and successful artist and craftsman.

Gill carved his first crucifixion in 1910, and went on to carve over fifty depictions in stone and wood both on commission and for himself. Judith Collins notes in her 1998 catalogue raisonné of Gill's sculpture that this relief was the first in which Gill depicted Christ with the crown of thorns, one of the symbols of the Passion. Gill depicted the image of Christ on the Cross in many different ways, including Christ the King, Christ in the action of Benediction, Christ as strong and therefore triumphant, as well as Christ as meek and therefore sacrificial.

Like many of Gill's sculptures, this piece is intended to be seen from only one perspective. Gill rarely carved sculptures in the round, possibly reflecting his training in letter cutting and his work as a wood engraver. Gill's use of colour was unusual in twentieth century sculpture, and was something he used in his inscriptions as well as his sculptures.

SANCTVS
CHRISTVS
DE
CAPEL-Y-FFIN

DAVID JONES (1895 – 1974)

SANCTUS CHRISTUS DE CAPEL-Y-FFIN
1925

Dr Richard Cork is a British art historian, editor, critic, broadcaster and exhibition curator. He has been an art critic for the *Evening Standard*, *The Listener*, *The Times* and the *New Statesman*. Cork was also editor for Studio International. He is a past Turner Prize judge.

At first sight, this heartfelt image seems rooted in David Jones' response to the Black Mountains. He had settled in Wales at the end of the previous year, arriving in December 1924 to join his friend Eric Gill and three families who had just moved from Sussex to a place dramatically high in the valley of the Honddu, north of Abergavenny. Here, in a former monastery at Capel-y-ffin, Jones felt that he had come home. His father's Welsh ancestry profoundly affected Jones' imagination, and in 1915 he had enlisted as a private in the Royal Welch Fusiliers. That is why, a decade later, he adapted with great eagerness to the immensity and remoteness of his new surroundings. As the title of this 1925 gouache proclaims, with its capital letters floating among the clouds, the dying martyr is identifiable as 'Sanctus Christus de Capel-y-ffin'. The wooden Cross, on which Jesus has been impaled with such relentless force, is clearly made of branches hewn from trees growing on the nearby mountain. Their raw stumps can be detected around the distant chapel. And, as Christ dangles painfully from the nails hammered into his hands, the horizontal branch stretching across the uppermost part of the picture shows no sign of weakening. It stays firm, while the bare trees beyond look equally resilient as they withstand the formidable rigours of a Welsh winter.

But Christ's own ability to endure should not be underestimated. Although blood spurts from the cruel gash in his side and runs down his feet as well, he possesses the sculptural solidity of a figure carved for a wayside shrine. He belongs to this ancient setting as much as the bird flying towards him, and his body fits into the deep fissures coursing down the mountainsides beyond.

Even so, the suffering endured by Jesus must also be intended as a war memorial. Jones never forgot the appalling violence inflicted on so many young men serving in the trenches. Their trauma was often likened to the Passion of Christ. And in 1937 he drew, as the frontispiece to his literary masterpiece *In Parenthesis*, a young soldier crucified in No Man's Land. However desperately wounded the infantryman might be, his body still echoes the obstinate strength of the stripped and battered trees around him. In this respect, Christ on the cross at Capel-y-ffin can be seen as the stoical redeemer of everyone who lost their lives in the battlefields of the First World War.

SYBIL ANDREWS (1898 – 1992)

GOLGOTHA 1931

ROWENA LOVERANCE IS A *BYZANTINE* ART HISTORIAN AND AUTHOR OF BYZANTIUM, AS WELL AS *CHRISTIAN ART*, A GLOBAL ACCOUNT OF CONTEMPORARY CULTURAL THEMES. ROWENA IS A LIFELONG QUAKER, AND HAS REPRESENTED THE SOCIETY OF FRIENDS IN ECUMENICAL AND INTERFAITH DIALOGUE FOR MANY YEARS.

To contemplate the Crucifixion rendered in linocut is to experience a degree of dislocation. Linocut is a self-deprecatory medium, usually associated with cheap materials and children's first efforts at printmaking. Is it really suited to representing such an overwhelming event?

In Sybil Andrews, though, we have a master of the medium. She first learned it in the late 1920s, at the Grosvenor School of Art, as a pupil of Futurist artist Claude Flight. After a decade working and exhibiting in London, she turned her hand to boat-building during the Second World War, and afterwards emigrated with her husband to Canada, to a remote logging town on Vancouver Island. Here she taught, and continued to produce linocuts, amassing about eighty in the course of her long life.

Golgotha is one of her early works. Although she has left no record of any religious beliefs, Andrews was clearly fascinated by the Christian story. The following year she made another Crucifixion, *Mother and Son*, in more conventional mourning colours of blue and purple, and in the 1950s a dramatic Stations of the Cross series.

Futurism sought to represent the speed and dynamism of the modern world, but Andrews was fascinated by the rhythm of the human figure, whether at work (*Winch*, 1930) or at play (*Racing*, 1934). One of her key compositional techniques of this period was to employ a single focal point as a pivot for the action. In *Golgotha*, the curvilinear forms of the mourning women in the lower register balance the angular forms of the crosses in the upper register, and the energy of the print is firmly focused on the point where the three crosses plunge into the rocky, unforgiving ground.

Sybil Andrews enjoyed the use of colour, comparing the different blocks to the four voice parts in a madrigal. But above all she enjoyed the use of line. She wrote: 'It is impossible to be fussy with lines, you have to simplify, you are forced to simplify your idea to its fundamentals'.

EWAS
A
THIEF
NRI

MICHAEL ROTHENSTEIN (1908 - 1993)

THE CRUCIFIXION 1937

Mel Gooding is an art critic, writer and exhibition organiser. His monographs on artists include Bruce McLean, Michael Rothenstein's Boxes, Patrick Heron, Gillian Ayres and Ceri Richards.

In this provocatively secular 'crucifixion', Michael Rothenstein has taken the subject as a means to express outrage at the suffering of ordinary people. It was painted at a time of great social and political turmoil: the Spanish Civil War was at its height, in 1938 came the betrayal of Czechoslovakia with the Munich Agreement and many were convinced of the inevitability of war with Nazi Germany. It was a dark time. Rothenstein was acutely aware of the currents of violence that flowed through these situations and events. Indeed the presence of violence haunted his artistic imagination until the end of his life.

The Crucifixion has long constituted an image of violence and human cruelty, and Rothenstein was well aware that artists (and writers) have often used biblical events and characters as metaphors for historical actualities. In his teens he had made a powerful drawing of *The Expulsion* (1925) that drew on Masaccio's famous image, and he made drawings of the *Deposition* and of *The Last Supper* in the early 1940s.

Rothenstein's treatment of the Crucifixion has a heightened theatricality, the viewpoint set at dynamic diagonal to the action which itself is staged in the immediate present with a cast drawn from contemporary life. The Christ-figure and the gagged figure to his left, and a slightly older man whose garb suggests him to be a professional of some kind - have been crucified. At the foot of the cross the wife or girlfriend of the central figure clings to his lifeless leg and a friend sets down a vase of spring flowers. In the foreground, respectable professional craftsmen prepare nonchalantly to leave, having accomplished their task. The very ordinariness of these characters adds a particular horror to the scene: in the world of the present - a world permeated by betrayal and violence - there are those who will perform these roles when the situation requires it. Another ladder, and the suggestion of a crowd in the background, suggests that this scene is being repeated elsewhere.

Jude

EMMANUEL LEVY (1900 – 1986)

CRUCIFIXION 1942

David Breuer-Weil is an artist and was Director of Impressionist and Modern art at Sotheby's. He also works as an art advisor and consultant.

Levy was by no means the only Jewish artist to use Christ as a Jewish symbol. From the 19th century onwards artists depicted him as a Jewish preacher (as in Maurycy Gottleib's *Christ Preaching in Capernaum*), a brilliant young scholar (Liebermann's *Jesus in the Synagogue*), as a Jewish national hero (Antokolski's sculpture of Christ), as a mystical visitor to the Polish ghetto (Wilhelm Wachtel's paintings of the subject) and as the victim of modern anti-Semitism in several works by Chagall.

Perhaps the only fact that is known for certainty about the historical Jesus is that he was a Jew, and an orthodox one at that. In Levy's *Crucifixion* this fact is represented by the phylacteries that Christ is wearing (these have been found in archaeological digs in Israel from the time of Christ). As in the images of Chagall, Levy wraps the victim in the Tallis, the Jewish prayer shawl. In this work Levy highlights the immense tragedy of the centuries of Jewish suffering caused in part by the misunderstanding of the nature of Christ's Jewish origins by the Church, and indeed the oft-repeated calumny that the Jews were responsible for Christ's death at the hand of the Roman procurator Pontius Pilate. Far from being responsible for Christ's death, the Jews are presented as synonymous with Christ as the scapegoat of Christian Europe. He is seen as an archetypal Jewish martyr. He is painted as Christ the victim of Rome and idolatry, as one of the countless victims of the Nazi genocide then raging in Europe.

"The thought 'we are being crucified' kept recurring to my mind over and over again until I was finally impelled to put the thought down on canvas. The initials INRI – a piece of Roman cynicism – have been replaced by the word Jude (German for Jew) written in blood, a truer and more terrifying fact thus bringing my conception into the twentieth century."

Levy painted this work in 1942, the year that witnessed a great number of victims of the Holocaust. It was at precisely that time that the gas chambers of Treblinka, Sobibor, Belzec and Auschwitz claimed the lives of the great majority of Eastern European Jewry. Levy seems to encapsulate that time in this single work.

DUNCAN GRANT (1885 - 1978)

DRAWING FOR THE BERWICK CRUCIFIXION

c. 1942

Richard Shone is Editor of *The Burlington Magazine* and has written on many aspects of twentieth-century British art. His first published catalogue was a history of the Berwick murals for an exhibition in Eastbourne in 1969. He is also author of *The Art of Bloomsbury: Roger Fry, Vanessa Bell, and Duncan Grant* and *Bloomsbury Portraits: Vanessa Bell, Duncan Grant and Their Circle.*

The ancient village church of St Michael and All Angels at Berwick in the South Downs was rudely awoken from its slumbers when the great Bishop Bell of Chichester put into action a plan to decorate its interior. The idea came about as part of his initiative to bring art and artists into closer contact with the Church. In the winter of 1939-40, Duncan Grant, with his collaborators, Vanessa Bell and her son Quentin Bell, all then living in war-time seclusion at Charleston, near to Berwick, drew up a scheme for decorations on both sides of the chancel arch and the north and south walls of the nave, with the possibility of later additions. The scheme soon ran into difficulties before it could be approved, through protests from some local parishioners. When these had eventually been overcome, a faculty of work was granted in 1941 and the paintings (oil on board) were installed in 1942. *Christ in Glory* by Grant looks down from the arch; on the reverse is Quentin Bell's *Parable of the Wise and Foolish Virgins*; and on the nave walls are a *Nativity* and an *Annunciation* by Vanessa Bell. This outcome is one of the most notable twentieth-century decorative schemes in a church and a vindication of Bishop Bell's patronage and enthusiasm.

The Charleston artists were by no means church-going Christians and had not previously attempted decorations on New Testament themes. But they took the Berwick commission completely seriously, fortified by their profound knowledge of the iconography of European religious painting. Later additions included Grant's *Crucifixion* at the west end of the church; his friend the painter Edward Le Bas posed for the figure of Christ 'tied to an easel' in the Charleston studio. The drawing for this, included in this exhibition, is among countless studies, drawn and painted, made by the artists in their thorough preparations for the final scheme.

ROY DE MAISTRE (1894 – 1968)

CRUCIFIXION 1942–44

Dr Heather Johnson is the author of two books on the artist Roy de Maistre and one on art patronage in Sydney. She has a PhD in Art History and Theory.

Roy de Maistre was born in New South Wales, Australia in 1894 and, having gained the reputation of being Australia's first abstract painter, won an art scholarship and travelled to Europe in 1923. On his return to Australia in 1925, he found the art community largely unsympathetic to abstract art, and modified his painting style to one of a decorative modernism, of stylised forms and colour – a style that formed the basis of his future oeuvre. In 1930 he returned to England and remained there for the rest of his life. He found a place among the English modernist painters, having work featured in the first edition of Herbert Read's *Art Now* and associated with the painters exhibiting at the Mayor Gallery. As well as his own work, de Maistre is often recognised for his formative influence on the painter, Francis Bacon.

De Maistre's faith was one of the most important aspects of his life and was well integrated into his art. From his earliest professional life, he was often described as having a 'spiritual' side to his nature, and in 1919 described colour in art as 'the spiritual speech of every living thing'. He was raised an Anglican, showed an interest in theosophy and anthroposophy during the 1920s, but found his spiritual home in Catholicism, converting to that faith in 1951.

The work in the exhibition, *The Crucifixion*, dated 1942/44 is one of several depictions the artist made of the crucifixion including within his *Stations of the Cross* in Westminster Cathedral. *The Crucifixion* focuses on the torso of Christ, and achieves a fine balance between passion and decorative control. The piercing lines and distorting geometric forms of the body not only convey the feeling of writhing agony but also give an impression of control and power. It also represents the complexity of de Maistre's deeply felt faith in Christ, not as meek and loving, but as a source of strength.

LEE MILLER (1907 – 1977)

HOTLINE TO GOD 1944

ANTONY PENROSE IS THE SON AND BIOGRAPHER OF LEE MILLER AND ROLAND PENROSE. HE IS DIRECTOR OF THE LEE MILLER ARCHIVES AND THE PENROSE COLLECTION WHICH ARE LOCATED IN HIS FAMILY HOME OF FARLEY FARM HOUSE, CHIDDINGLY, EAST SUSSEX WHICH HAS BECOME A MUSEUM DEDICATED TO THE WORK OF HIS PARENTS.

The fighting front has moved forward from this location in Strasbourg, but the sporadic shell bursts that still shatter the city have sheared the top of the cross. The advancing Signal Corps linesmen have reeled out their phone cables in a looping cat's cradle using the cross as a telegraph pole. It is November 1944, and Strasbourg has been liberated by the Free French and the US Army.

Lee Miller's career began as a cover girl for *Vogue Magazine* in 1927 and she was now a combat photographer for the same magazine, following the US Army across Europe since soon after D Day. Before the war she had lived in Paris working with the American Surrealist photographer Man Ray. This moment was precious to her as the German invaders were about to be finally driven from the country she had come to love.

With Man Ray's encouragement she became a Surrealist photographer in her own right, and many of her war reportage images contain Surrealist metaphors. The Surrealists loved the found object (*l'objet trouvé*), something found by chance they felt contained the marvellous. For Lee Miller it was the found image (*l'image trouvé*) that interested her and the destruction of war provided a rich crop for her unerring eye. In her Surrealist work her intention was to provoke rather inform, to raise questions and stimulate the viewer. Is the way the lines snake off on all directions a symbol of the importance of communication? Is the way the cables have caught and held the broken fragment of the cross a symbol of how by communicating we can save our civilisation from destruction? Is the way the wooden pole bends under the weight of the lines yet the stone cross endures a metaphor for the endurance of our culture despite the transience of organic things? Lee Miller leaves you to choose and to find your own meanings.

Chagall

MARC CHAGALL (1887 – 1985)

APOCALYPSE EN LILAS, CAPRICCIO 1945

JACKIE WULLSCHLAGER, AUTHOR OF *CHAGALL: LOVE AND EXILE*, IS CHIEF ART CRITIC OF THE *FINANCIAL TIMES* – THIS TEXT IS A SHORTENED, ADAPTED VERSION OF A REVIEW ON 16 JANUARY 2010. HER BOOKS INCLUDE *HANS CHRISTIAN ANDERSEN: THE LIFE OF A STORYTELLER* AND A GROUP BIOGRAPHY OF VICTORIAN CHILDERN'S WRITERS, *INVENTING WONDERLAND*.

This anguished gouache, ink and pencil Crucifixion in grey and lilac is Chagall' s most immediate response to the images of the Holocaust which emerged in spring 1945; it is unlike anything else he ever painted and startlingly different from his mostly whimsical, nostalgic 1940s works.

His title, *Apocalypse in Lilac, Capriccio*, expresses the work's arresting mix of terror, discord and beauty. A naked Christ confronts a blackened Nazi soldier crouching in animal pose as he attempts to remove the ladder from the cross. The Nazi's hand has been amputated but his serpent's tail trails threateningly around a mother and child group. Around them are not only Chagall's typical symbols of Jewish suffering – Jew clutching a Torah scroll, woman with hands outstretched, boatload of refugees – but a cluster of images of naked victims, skeletal and traumatised, by a camp fence, and a series of hanged and crucified figures amid burning buildings. Their directness, brutality and nudity, exceptional in Chagall's oeuvre, leave no doubt that they were inspired by Holocaust photographs. A grandfather clock, a familiar Chagall motif, falls, upside down, from the sky; its minute and hour hands are missing, and appear as sketches nearby: the end of time.

This is the bleakest of Chagall's many Crucifixions. Nowhere else did he combine symbols with realistic images as in *Apocalypse in Lilac, Capriccio*, nor horror with such tenderness. Christ's hips curve sensually like a woman's, and recall Chagall's depictions of wife Bella, who had died six months earlier. His recurring images of Bella as bride are also echoed in the full-length white prayer shawl coursing down Christ's back like a bridal gown, and suggest this as a very personal mourning picture as well as a universal one. Chagall's urgency, unhappiness and raw approach – fragmented lines, erasures, overpainting – are palpable. But as strong is the master's hand – the controlled composition, the finely judged soft greys, pale lilac, velvet blacks – give a grave delicacy to this marvellous piece.

ROBERT HENDERSON BLYTH (1919 – 1970)

IN THE IMAGE OF MAN 1947

DUNCAN MACMILLAN IS PROFESSOR EMERITUS OF THE HISTORY OF SCOTTISH ART AND AN HONORARY ROYAL SCOTTISH ACADEMICIAN. HE IS CURATOR OF THE ROYAL SOCIETY OF EDINBURGH AND FORMER CURATOR OF THE TALBOT RICE GALLERY, THE UNIVERSITY OF EDINBURGH. HE IS ART CRITIC OF *THE SCOTSMAN* AND AUTHOR OF A NUMBER OF BOOKS INCLUDING *SCOTTISH ART 1460–2000* AND *SCOTTISH ART IN THE 20TH CENTURY*.

Robert Henderson Blyth trained at Glasgow School of Art, but he found the work of James Cowie, whom he encountered at Hospitalfield, the Scottish Art Colleges' summer school, more sympathetic than that of his Glasgow teachers. Cowie was a great draughtsman. He also had a very individual approach to symbolism and so perhaps his influence is reflected in the extraordinary symbolism of this picture. If God made man in his image, what wreckage has man made in his own?

Henderson Blyth was enlisted in the Royal Army Medical Corps in 1941 and after D-Day went with the invading army through France and Belgium into Germany. In 1946, immediately after he was demobbed, he was appointed to teach at Edinburgh College of Art. Later he moved from Edinburgh to teach at Gray's School of Art in Aberdeen. Elizabeth Blackadder was taught and influenced by him at Edinburgh. She also knew him when his memories of the war were still fresh and remembers that he did not disguise how much he was affected by his war experiences.

In addition to *In the Image of Man*, there are several others that are testimony to the truth of her recollection. There is a portrait in the Scottish National Gallery of Modern Art, which may be of the artist himself, standing in a shell-hole, behind is a fallen comrade covered in snow. There is also an extraordinary painting in a private collection of shattered railway wagons and twisted lines painted when Henderson Blyth's unit was stationed in the city of Hamburg which had been completely devastated by RAF bombers. To judge by the wide flat landscape beyond the ruined town, Hamburg also seems likely to be the setting for *In the Image of Man*. If that is so, the main point of the picture and of its title is a terrible irony. This awful devastation was wrought by the Allies in the name of civilisation, of humanity, or, if you will, in the image of man.

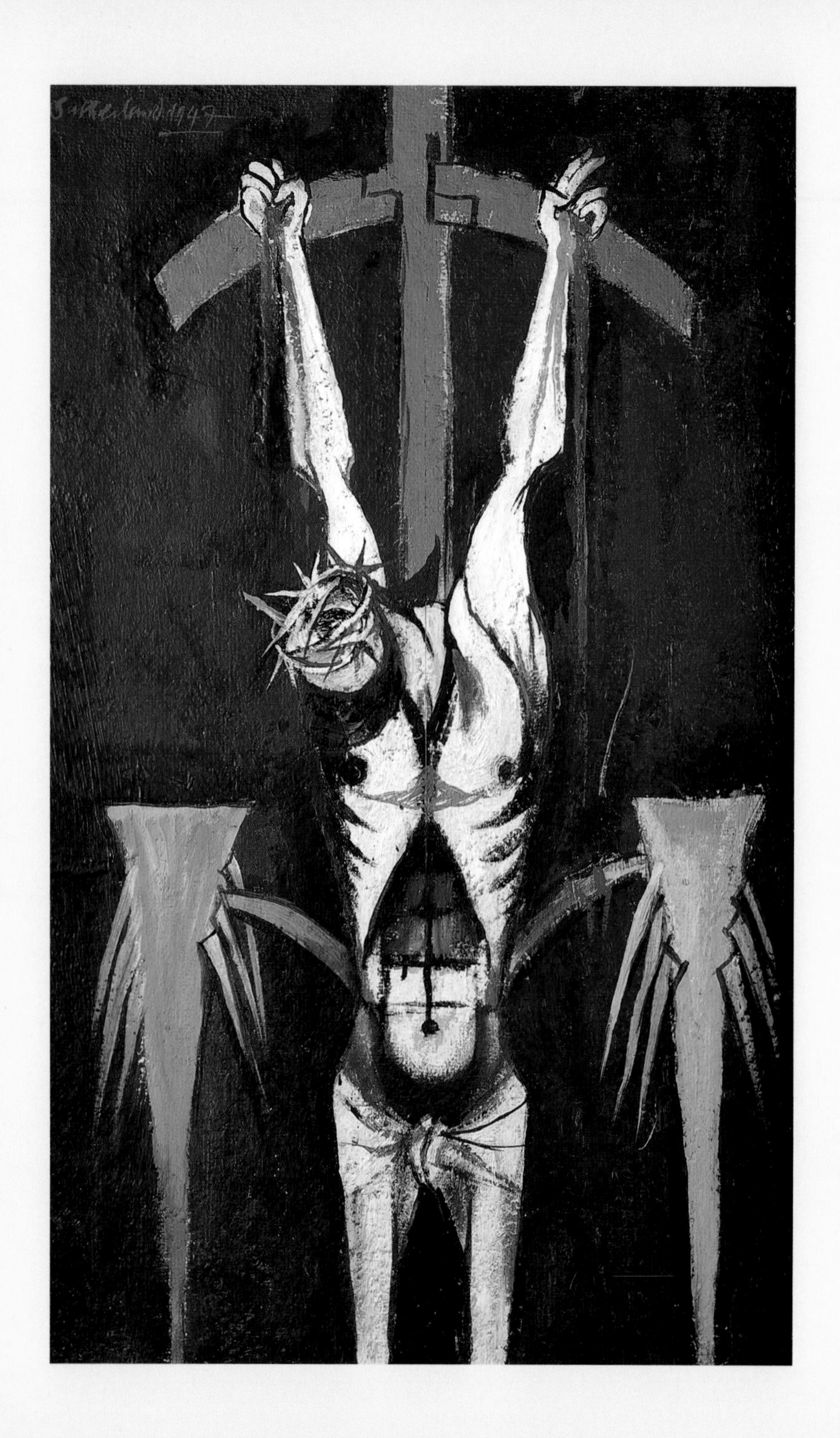

GRAHAM SUTHERLAND (1903 - 1980)

CRUCIFIXION 1947

MARTIN HAMMER IS READER IN HISTORY OF ART AT THE UNIVERSITY OF EDINBURGH, AND HIS BOOKS INCLUDE *BACON AND SUTHERLAND* AND *GRAHAM SUTHERLAND: LANDSCAPES, WAR SCENES AND PORTRAITS 1924–1950.*

Graham Sutherland's variations on the theme of the Crucifixion were a by-product of his commission to produce a large picture for St Matthew's, Northampton, to hang opposite Henry Moore's *Madonna and Child* sculpture. He had been approached in 1944 by Reverend Walter Hussey. Hussey suggested an *Agony in the Garden* for his church, but the artist preferred to do a Crucifixion. In this he epitomised a widespread impulse during the Second World War to employ this theme as a powerful distillation of the murderous violence and cruelty that an ascendant Fascism had inflicted upon Europe.

For an artist who had specialised in modestly sized landscapes, it proved a challenge to achieve a comparable intensity with figurative imagery, on a monumental scale and for a public setting. Meanwhile his immersion in Crucifixion imagery found an outlet in his *Thorn Tree* and *Thorn Head* pictures, where he projected cruelty onto the spiky forms of nature. It took Sutherland more than two and a half years to produce the picture for St Matthew's, which was unveiled in November 1946. His main point of departure for the final image was the great *Isenheim Altarpiece* by Matthias Grünewald, Sutherland's "favourite painter". But he was also stimulated by his friendship with Francis Bacon, whose career was launched in spring 1945 by the famous triptych *Three Studies for Figures at the base of a Crucifixion* (1944). Moreover, while contemplating the project, Sutherland saw photographs of the piles of splayed corpses at Belsen: "the whole idea of the depiction of Christ crucified became much more real to me... and it seemed to be possible to do this subject again." The experience reinforced Sutherland's willingness to treat the body of Christ as emaciated and distorted by agony, which is especially evident in the several independent spin-off pictures that he now produced, including the Chichester picture formerly owned by Hussey. One critic felt that The Crucifixion had lost its consoling or redemptive force in Sutherland's hands: "in the agony of Christ's martyrdom on the Cross, Sutherland voices the present crisis in civilisation".

JOHN ARMSTRONG (1893 – 1973)

CRUCIFIXION 1958

ANDREW LAMBIRTH IS A WRITER AND CURATOR, CURRENTLY ART CRITIC FOR *THE SPECTATOR*. HE HAS WRITTEN FOR A WIDE RANGE OF PUBLICATIONS INCLUDING *THE ART NEWSPAPER*, *MODERN PAINTERS*, *THE INDEPENDENT* AND *THE SUNDAY TIMES*. HIS MANY BOOKS ON BRITISH ARTISTS INCLUDE *ROGER HILTON*, *CRAIGIE AITCHISON: OUT OF THE ORDINARY*, *KITAJ*, *MAGGI HAMBLING* AND *JOHN ARMSTRONG*.

John Armstrong said that as a child he loved everything that was painted because it was not real, and his mature vision as an artist offers remarkable confirmation of his belief in the power and authority of the imagination. Even before the savage bombing of the Second World War he painted a civilisation in ruins, and his post-war imagery became increasingly apocalyptic. Hovering between disillusionment and satire, Armstrong employed intense symbolic imagery to convey the sense of threat he felt in a nuclear age. Armstrong's widow considers that he was religious by temperament, though he rebelled against his Church of England upbringing as the son of a clergyman: 'He was committed to the concept of belief and the necessity to prove it in action. In his painting and the themes that obsessed him he was absorbed by this reality.'

Crucifixion was painted for 'The Religious Theme', a Contemporary Art Society exhibition. Christ is quietly depicted, the drama reserved for the mourners who in their different coloured robes are arranged compositionally around a series of dynamic triangles (neatly symbolising the Trinity). The most powerful of these is formed by the three fists at bottom right, convulsively clutching at garments. It is a highly effective evocation of anguish and suffering, the extremes of feeling concisely conveyed. All three faces are turned away in the privacy of emotion, the central figure reaching up towards Christ in a gesture which suggests both earthly yearning and the ascension of the departing spirit. Contemporary commentators found the painting compelling and sincere without being theatrical.

Crucifixion was painted three years after Armstrong parted acrimoniously from his second wife, and it is unquestionably informed by the depth of emotional upset that event caused. By 1958, the artist had met Annette Heaton, the woman who was to become his third wife, and his life was returning to an even keel, but he had learnt much about suffering. That understanding helps to account for the power of this image: Armstrong found a way of transmuting his personal hurt into a religious image of considerable potency.

STANLEY SPENCER (1891 – 1959)

DRAWINGS FOR THE CRUCIFIXION 1958

RICHARD MARTINEAU WAS A BREWER AND, SINCE RETIRING, HAS FARMED IN SUFFOLK. HE IS A PAST CHAIRMAN OF THE ROYAL SOCIETY OF ARTS AND WAS DEPUTY CHAIRMAN OF LONDON UNIVERSITY'S INSTITUTE OF EDUCATION AND A SYNDIC ON CAMBRIDGE UNIVERSITY'S EXAM BOARD. HE WAS ALSO ON THE NATIONAL LOTTERY CHARITY BOARD.

The Crucifixion, Stanley's last completed work, was commissioned by my father, John Martineau. We lived about five miles from Cookham and my mother, wishing to have a drawing of me, was introduced to Stanley in 1943. He arrived wearing his pyjama trousers under his ordinary ones and from that moment became a family friend.

My mother was worried that he did not look after himself and would often ask him to Sunday lunch 'to feed him up for the week ahead'. One day in the summer of 1957 I went to collect him for one such lunch. I found him sitting on a chair placed on top of a table working on *Christ Preaching at Cookham*. While I waited I looked through some drawers in a chest where he kept drawing of ideas for future paintings – one was of a crucifixion. I took the drawing with me back to my parents and said that I hoped someone would commission the painting while Stanley was still well enough to paint it.

My father was a brewer and had been painted by Stanley as Master of the Brewers Company in 1955. He was also Chairman of the Board of Governors of Aldenham School which was supported by the Brewers Company. He agreed to commission the painting for the school chapel. At that time main drainage was being installed in Cookham and a large mound of excavated earth outside Stanley's window became the hill of Calvary.

At the dedication service Stanley told the boys that 'I have given the men nailing Christ to the Cross (and making sure they make a good job of it) – Brewers' Caps – because it is your Governors, and you, who are still nailing Christ to the Cross'. When it came to be sold at Sotheby's in 1990 there was a strong contingent from Cookham able to identify the originals for both the crucifiers and the onlookers. Stanley was reputed to have said to one of Cookham's more disreputable characters: 'I've got you'.

F N SOUZA (1924 - 2002)

CRUCIFIXION 1959

PARTHA MITTER IS PROFESSOR EMERITUS IN ART HISTORY, UNIVERSITY OF SUSSEX. BOOKS INCLUDE *MUCH MALIGNED MONSTERS: HISTORY OF EUROPEAN REACTIONS TO INDIAN ART, ART AND NATIONALISM IN COLONIAL INDIA 1850-1922,* AND *THE TRIUMPH OF MODERNISM: INDIA'S ARTISTS AND THE AVANT-GARDE 1922-1947.*

The most controversial member of the Progressive Artists Group of Bombay founded in 1947, the Goanese painter Francis Newton Souza launched his artistic career with a nude self-portrait calculated to outrage the citizens of Bombay. In the words of their mentor Rudi von Leyden, Souza and the Progressives asserted "that great emotional power and significance is contained in the very elements of painting, namely colour and form, and they can be used almost in the pure abstract state to convey the feelings or ideas of the artist." Souza once claimed that his painting was a product of his libido and is perhaps best known for a series of sexually charged nudes that drew upon the erotic art of the Hindu temples. However, arguably his most powerful works are those which deal with Christian themes.

The savage and excruciating treatment of *Crucifixion* both moves and repulses as it invites us to share the agony of the persecuted Christ much in the manner of Grünewald's great crucifixion on the Isenheim Altarpiece. Souza's spikey forms resemble trees with thorns. The Saviour's face is a 'primitive' mask while the primal quality of the composition is complemented by thick black lines, the metallic blue and the sickly orange.

A lapsed Catholic, Souza had ambivalent relationship with the Church. While his early communist leanings made him reject the hypocrisy of its clergy and its oppressive institutional aspects (as parodied in his paintings of grotesque popes and saints), Souza obsessively returns to the image of the suffering Christ as personifying the alienation of modernity. Indeed, in his last painting, he pointedly identifies Christ with the suffering city-dweller of Bombay. Souza's tortured canvases depicting extremes of pain, such as *Crucifixion*, are not only moving for their visceral imagination, but also because of his preoccupation with the formal values of painting, what he termed the significant form. It is this combination of the 'primitive' quality of drawing and the garish primary colours that make his Christian art contemporary as well as compelling.

CRAIGIE AITCHISON (1926 - 2009)

CRUCIFIXION IX 1963

Christopher Irvine, Canon Librarian at Canterbury Cathedral, is a trustee of Art and Christian Enquiry, and is the author of *The Art of God*. He is currently researching images of the cross as the tree of life.

As a student at the Slade, Aitchison received criticism for painting a copy of a Rouault crucifixion, and was told that it was too serious a subject for him to paint. But he soon found his own individual style of using of colour, shape and form to paint his distinctive crucifixions which he painted throughout his life. Within Aitchison's crucifixions, the cross appears like a question-mark set in a landscape that is often inspired by the hills of Tuscany. As one would expect from an artist who is reticent about the meanings of his paintings, these question-marks pose gentle, almost quizzical questions about life and death, rather than being statements of conventional religious meaning. The composition occasionally includes one of his beloved Bedlington terriers, or a colourful bird or two, but generally, the figure is alone, almost marginal. Essentially the figure is set in a tranquil banded field of colour, and it is the colouring that is so distinctive of Craigie's paintings. The palette is always of single, unmixed, warm and tranquil colours.

In this early painting of the cross, the composition of the crucified is the Gothic Y figure. The arms hang down from the horizontal cross beam, holding the dead weight of the body, and yet the body (and the wisp of a loin cloth) is iridescent with a white light. The lonely figure of Aitchison's crucifixions recalls the haunting cry of *Lamentation* 'Look, and see if there is any sorrow like my sorrow' and yet, as the finely painted white lines and the star above the head indicate, the human figure of the Crucified is also a site of a mysterious transfiguration, of a divine splendour suffusing and transfiguring the human figure. What strikes the viewer in this dynamic crucifixion painting is not a body abandoned, but a body being transformed, and transformed with the same light and energy which shines through the artist's portrait paintings, which reveal a wonderful depth of individual presence and the 'human form divine'.

BETTY SWANWICK (1915 – 1989)

THE LOST WILDERNESS 1974

PADDY ROSSMORE READ THEOLOGY AT TRINITY COLLEGE, CAMBRIDGE. AFTER FARMING IN IRELAND HE BECAME INTERESTED IN PSYCHOTHERAPY AND, IN 1973, CO-FOUNDED A THERAPEUTIC COMMUNITY NEAR DUBLIN. ROSSMORE WAS A CLOSE FRIEND OF BETTY SWANWICK, COLLECTOR OF HER WORK, AND IS AUTHOR OF HER BIOGRAPHY AND CATALOGUE RAISONNÉ PUBLISHED BY CHRIS BEETLES GALLERY IN 2008.

Having worked as an illustrator during the first part of her professional career, Betty Swanwick then started an extraordinary series of visionary paintings that she continued until the end of her life. These works parallel a present day movement to recognise an inner form of Christianity of psychological enlightenment and spiritual meaning. She painted many pictures with references to biblical stories – what she called "biblical goings-on". Their themes could be prophetic and are probably ahead of their time. *The Lost Wilderness* is one of the series.

This picture, sometimes referred to as *The Wilderness Lost*, has an accompanying picture *The Wilderness Regained*, so suggesting a reference to Milton. Nowadays we see wilderness areas as places undisturbed by man and they would have a special meaning for Swanwick who was a great lover of animals, gardens and the natural world.

In *The Lost Wilderness* the figures in the background display feelings of despair and frustration. The foreground figure, seemingly a part of the tree, suggests to us a crucifixion. The ground is littered with empty cans and bottles, the excesses of a man made world. This powerful picture evokes a wasteland, a world devastated for the animals as well as for humankind.

This leads to another level of meaning where the picture is a depiction of a state of consciousness, that of alienation, where a feeling of divine support is no longer experienced, echoing the words from the cross "Why hast Thou forsaken me?" Besides, however, the despair and devastation, a pointing finger of one of the man's hands directs our attention downwards. The foxes, perhaps representing new life, are stirring after sleep amongst the intricate and sensitively drawn roots of the tree.
Betty Swanwick taught at Goldsmiths' College School of Art, where she had formerly been a student, for almost 40 years. She lived with her cats, dogs and parrot in Greenwich and later Tunbridge Wells. Swanwick excelled at design and composition. She said she wanted to employ traditional disciplines in her work because they were tried and tested. As an artist her vision showed her to be an instinctive explorer of the psyche or soul who always remained close to the earth.

The Disposition 6/12/89

TRACEY EMIN (1963 –)

THE DISPOSITION 1989

Neal Brown is an artist and writer. He is the author of *Tracey Emin and Billy Childish, A Short Study*. He curated *To the Glory of God: New Religious Art* at the 2002 Liverpool Biennial.

Tracey Emin came to prominence in a 1990's art world that was much defined by its interest in irreligious religion, and there are different ways to interpret her decision to withhold showing the many works she had made that depict unambiguously Christian subjects. Finally, in 2002, she showed *The Disposition* and other similarly related pieces. (Emin's spelling of 'Disposition' is a deliberately preserved misspelling of deposition – the taking down of Jesus Christ from the cross). These works were disruptive of usual ideas of Emin's practice, and it is an irony that Emin probably required more courage to show these than her more usual themes.

The Disposition still commands power, but somewhat differently. We can now appreciate its more intrinsic merits, rather than its relationship with media driven agendas of shock and counter-shock, and we can even attempt to situate it in different lineages – lineages that might include the painter Albert Herbert, for example. The Crucifixion of Christ is a subject consistent with Emin's wide spiritual interests, and her practice is replete with examples of tragedy, sorrow and misfortune, from whose lamentations she salvages redemptive, spiritual possibility and ideas of afterlife.

Emin's *Disposition* is based, loosely, on early Byzantine crucifixion depictions, to which she gives an unexpected emphasis by showing Jesus more than once. Intensity is conferred by Emin's use of a transparent, but knotted linearity, through which the protagonists appear (at least at first viewing), to be almost coequal; a unity of pain, difficulty and compassion, rather than occupying their usually designated places of moral or spiritual hierarchy. (Usual iconographic hierarchies are further disrupted because *Disposition* is a monoprint, whose drawing technique requires image reversal). In this way Emin explores – even conflates – the enormous individual and social energies around the meaning of suffering, and successfully creates a sense of universal totality.

NORMAN ADAMS (1927 – 2005)

GOLDEN CRUCIFIXION 1993

SISTER WENDY BECKETT IS A CARMELITE NUN AND THE POPULAR HOST OF A VARIETY OF BBC TELEVISION SERIES, INCLUDING *SISTER WENDY'S ODYSSEY*, *SISTER WENDY'S GRAND TOUR*, AND *THE STORY OF PAINTING*. SHE IS THE AUTHOR OF NUMEROUS BOOKS ON RELIGIOUS ART AND NOW LIVES IN A CARAVAN IN THE GROUNDS OF A MONASTERY IN NORFOLK.

The crucifixion is not the central teaching of the Christian Faith. The centre of the Faith is the Resurrection. This is not apparent visually, because it is the cross that is the ubiquitous sign of the Church, and we can realise why. Death, even as horrible a death as crucifixion, is something we can understand, whereas resurrection is not. We know that Christ rose, but we cannot imagine how. But since crucifixion is merely a prologue to the glory of resurrection, it is the greatest joy to find an artist who can actually make both prologue and climax simultaneously visible. El Greco could do this and so can Norman Adams.

His *Golden Crucifixion* is a most extraordinary depiction of Christ both dying and rising into His divine splendour. The wood of the cross is being subsumed by the golden light of divinity. And behind His hanging body, and cart-wheeling around Him, are the magnificence of butterfly wings. It is as if life is a chrysalis, and we hatch out as Jesus does, into the full sunlight of butterfly freedom. The wings are studded with occluded suns. Balls of scarlet light float at will within a connecting nexus of white tendrils that link the world together, now that Jesus has united it by His sacrificial love.

Excluded from this liberating happiness, are the two gendarme figures on the left, authority clutching its weapons, and obstinately blind to the great reality behind them. They will not see. The two mourners on the left have not yet seen, because, temporarily, they are blinded by grief. The only one with a dawning realisation of what the Crucifixion means, is the Mary Madeline figure stretching out her arms in the classic resurrection gesture, that will bring from Jesus the gentle instruction: noli me tangere. Yet Adams shows her stretching out those longing arms, not to Jesus on the cross, but to the new brightness and freedom, the golden salvation, that He has won for us.

SAMUEL BAK (1933 –)

STUDY I 1995

THIS TEXT IS AN EXCERPT FROM *ICON OF LOSS: RECENT PAINTINGS BY SAMUEL BAK* WRITTEN IN 2008 BY DANNA NOLAN FEWELL, PROFESSOR OF HEBREW BIBLE AT DREW UNIVERSITY IN MADISON, NEW JERSEY AND GARY A. PHILLIPS, DEAN OF THE COLLEGE AND PROFESSOR OF RELIGION AT WABASH COLLEGE IN CRAWFORDSVILLE, INDIANA.

Samuel Bak was born in 1933 in Vilna, Poland and at the age of 7, as the town came under German occupation, Bak and his family moved into the Vilna ghetto, and later to a labor camp, from which he was smuggled and given refuge in a monastery. Bak has spent his life dealing with the artistic expression of the destruction and dehumanization which make up his childhood memories.

In *Study I* from 1995, Samuel Bak uses a documentary photograph of a young boy being held at gunpoint by a Nazi soldier as his subject to explore themes of survival and crucifixion. In the figure of the boy, the human and the inhuman collide. This unknown boy's isolation and outwardly-turned palms are a mimicry of crucifixion iconography, the boy appears to be reaching out to God, desiring, pleading for life in the face of imminent death. As Bak observes, "Arms that reach for the sky are also a gesture of surrender, of giving up. When you superimpose the image of a crucified Son on that of the little Warsaw boy with his uplifted arms, you are made to wonder, Where is God the Father?"

As viewers we peer into cracks on canvas, fractures in memory, and see a boy who becomes a threshold that guides us into a fragmentary past that resists being remade whole. This anguished manifestation of the boy brings us to the precipice of the present where we are confronted with the ways we fashion our children in our own image, saddling them both with our religious ideas and expectations and our propensity to solve all problems with violence. Bak invites us to become a community committed to living with ghosts, with loss. How do we now respond for all of the children, past and present, who risk oblivion? How do we journey forth in search of *tikkun olam* [a repaired world] with such ragged holes at the core of our world?

MAGGI HAMBLING (1945 –)

GOOD FRIDAY 2002

ANDREW LAMBIRTH IS A WRITER AND CURATOR, CURRENTLY ART CRITIC FOR *THE SPECTATOR*. HE HAS WRITTEN FOR A WIDE RANGE OF PUBLICATIONS INCLUDING *THE ART NEWSPAPER, MODERN PAINTERS, THE INDEPENDENT* AND *THE SUNDAY TIMES*. HIS MANY BOOKS ON BRITISH ARTISTS INCLUDE *ROGER HILTON, CRAIGIE AITCHISON: OUT OF THE ORDINARY, KITAJ, MAGGI HAMBLING* AND *JOHN ARMSTRONG*.

Every Good Friday, the artist Maggi Hambling composes herself to bear witness to Christ's Passion through her work. It is her habit to make a painting, drawing or sculpture on this theme, to focus on the revealed truths of Christ's life and death through the act of contemplation which is the essence of making art. This is the only time of the year that she gives herself up entirely to such subject matter, and though the thought that goes into the making of a piece may well overlap the one day, or indeed its casting (if it is in bronze) may take longer than a day to achieve, it is important to her that the activity remains focused on Good Friday.

It comes as a surprise to those who see only the witty, audacious and life-loving artist in the public eye to learn that Hambling has this thoughtful and spiritual side, but it is just such qualities which account for the depth and resonance of her work. She made her first painting of Jesus in 1965, while a student at Camberwell School of Art, a boldly patterned composition owing a good deal to the colouristic influences of Matisse and Yves Klein. Ten years later, she attempted to paint Christ and the Devil from the same model, but not surprisingly the paintings didn't work. She made her first *Good Friday* painting in 1986, partly as a tribute to her mother who was growing frail, and since then it has become a yearly ritual. When asked whether she is a believer, she calls herself 'an optimistic doubter'. She was brought up in the Church of England and attended church every Sunday. As she says: 'Consequently it is very difficult for me to think of anything else on Good Friday but the Crucifixion. The mystery. The sacrifice. The simultaneous death and life, and vice versa.'

The painting here emphasizes Christ's loneliness in His final moments. Although there are two other crosses evident, they are shadowy and seemingly untenanted. The vastness of the yellow-grey sky presses remorselessly down on the tiny figure who supports all this immensity on his bowed shoulders. It is a moving but affirmative image.

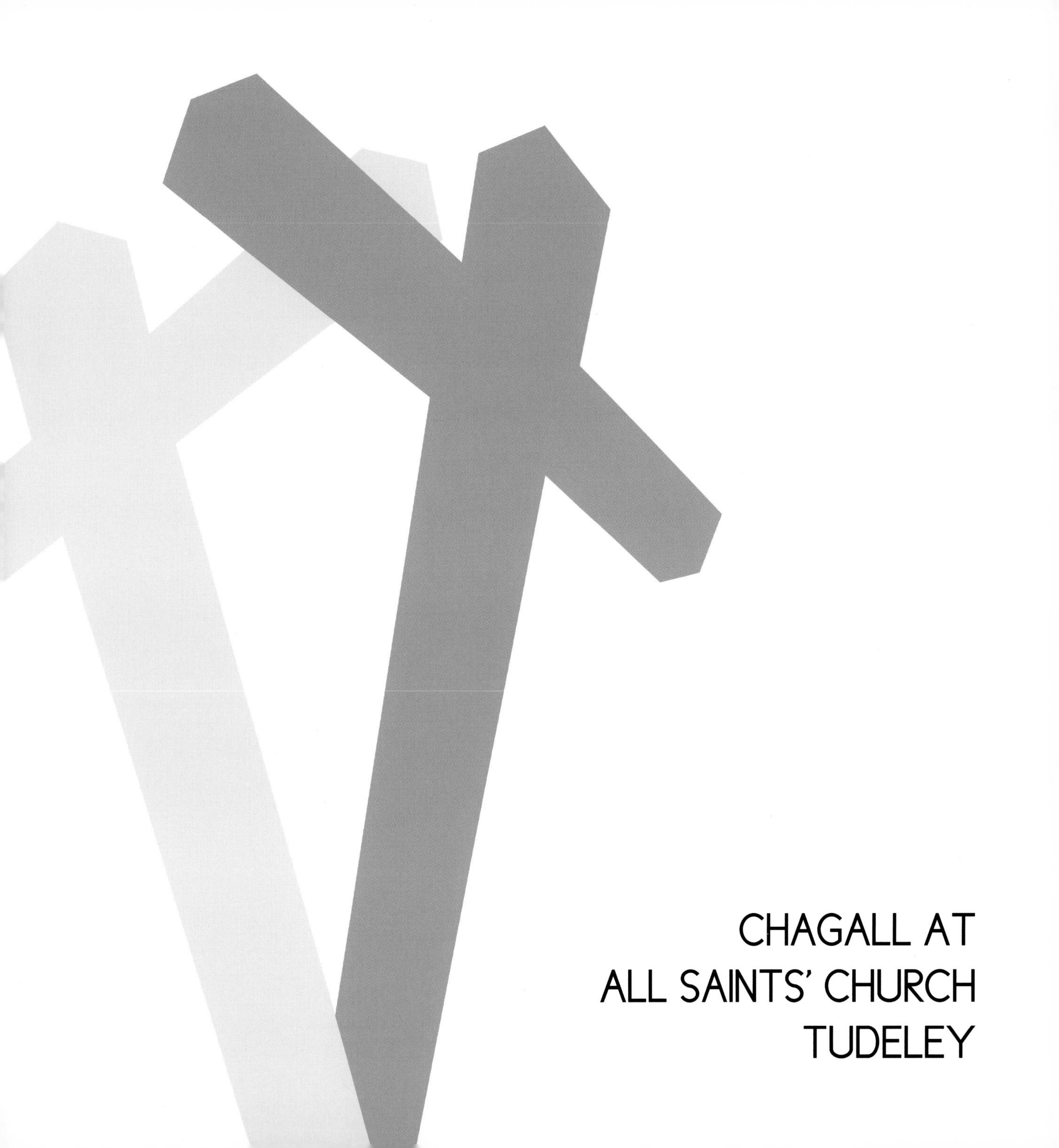

CHAGALL AT ALL SAINTS' CHURCH TUDELEY

IMAGES OF JESUS IN THE WORK OF MARC CHAGALL: CHRISTIAN REDEEMER OR JEWISH MARTYR?

BY MONICA BOHM-DUCHEN

MONICA BOHM-DUCHEN, AN INDEPENDENT ART HISTORIAN BASED IN LONDON, IS AUTHOR OF A MONOGRAPH ON CHAGALL, PUBLISHED BY PHAIDON IN 1998 AND REPRINTED IN 2001. OTHER PUBLICATIONS INCLUDE *RUBIES AND REBELS: JEWISH FEMALE IDENTITY IN CONTEMPORARY BRITISH ART* AND *THE ART AND LIFE OF JOSEF HERMAN.*

Born in 1887 into a poor but fervent Hasidic Jewish family living in Vitebsk in present-day Belarus, the Old Testament formed an intimate and integral part of Marc Chagall's upbringing. Although he soon ceased to be an observant Jew, the emphasis put by Hasidic Judaism – in contrast to orthodox Talmudic Judaism – on an intuitive, almost sensual communion with God undoubtedly played an important part in shaping his attitudes towards religion, life and art alike.

The Old Testament's continuing influence on Chagall during a career that spanned eight decades is borne out not only by his many works on Biblical themes but by ample written testimony, poems as well as prose. Unburdened by a Christian sense of original sin, Chagall's vision of the Bible, even when expressed on a small-scale, was of a grand human narrative of epic proportions, dominated by lofty emotions – be they tragic, ecstatic or even, occasionally, mixed with humour. As the artist himself put it: "I went to the great universal book, the Bible. Since my childhood it has filled me with visions about the fate of the world and inspired me in my work. In moments of doubt, its highly poetic grandeur and wisdom have comforted me like a second nature".

It was not only the Old Testament which haunted him. As even a cursory glimpse at almost any of the artist's images of his home town will confirm; its skyline dominated not only by the Uspensky Cathedral but by numerous baroque churches. The Christian Church – both literally and psychologically – was a constant presence, both framing and shaping his sense of identity. Chagall, in his own words, "had long been troubled by the pale face of Christ", and first treated the Crucifixion theme in 1913, in a striking but enigmatic work called *Dedicated to Christ*, later re-named *Golgotha* and later still, *Calvary*. Other early works making sly and somewhat subversive reference to the Christian tradition include *The Family or Maternity* (also known as *Circumcision*) of 1909, *The Holy Family* of 1910 and *Pregnant Woman or Maternity* of 1913.

In works such as these the Jewish references are only oblique. With the rise of Nazism in the 1930s and the implementation of the Final Solution (the Jewish population of Vitebsk was liquidated soon after the German invasion of Russia in 1941), the identification of Jesus as the original Jewish martyr and embodiment of Jewish suffering in the twentieth century, became almost an obsession for Chagall. The inclusion in *Cross Purposes* of Emanuel Levy's *Crucifixion* of 1942 bares out the fact that Chagall was by no means the only Jewish artist to make this identification. Non-Jewish artists such as Graham Sutherland, in his Crucifixion paintings of the late 1940s, would also make that uncomfortable connection; while as early as 1937, a Jesuit priest could write: "Like Jesus, the Jews have not ceased to mount Golgotha; like him, they are always nailed to the cross". After the war, the analogy between the martyrdom of Christ and that of the Jews became almost commonplace: indeed, when Dachau was liberated, the road through the camp was re-named "The Way of the Cross"; while Pope John Paul II could refer to Auschwitz as "the modern Golgotha". This identification was given further credibility by the terrible photographs and film footage that emerged of concentration camp victims, many of them frozen in poses reminiscent of the crucified Christ.

In *White Crucifixion* of 1938, the earliest and probably most powerful example of this obsession, Christ's Jewishness is established beyond question by the Jewish prayer-shawl he wears as a loin-cloth; while the scenes of Jewish suffering that surround him can all be linked to specific contemporary events.

MARC CHAGALL *YELLOW CRUCIFIXION* 1942

MARC CHAGALL *CRUCIFIXION* 1972

Many other Crucifixion images were to follow, especially after 1941, when Chagall was forced to seek refuge in the USA: among them, *Descent from the Cross* of 1941 (in which, contentiously, the artist replaced the words INRI with the initials of his own name – one of several canvases where the self-identification with Christ's suffering, intensified by the tragic death in 1944 of his beloved wife Bella, is made explicit); *Yellow Crucifixion* of 1943 (in which Christ wears phylacteries and an open Torah scroll covers his right arm), and *The Crucified* of 1944 (in which Christ is depicted as an eastern European Jew in a Jewish village street). Chagall's poems of this period confirm that for him, Jesus was indeed a Jew and a brother: "A Jew passes with the face of Christ/He cries: Calamity is upon us/Let us run and hide in the ditches"..."Day and Night I carry a Cross/I am shoved, dragged by the hand/Already Night surrounds me. And you/Abandon me, O God. Why?"

In the post-war period, as the trauma of the Holocaust and personal loss receded, the artist's references to Jesus for the most part became more generalised and less emotionally loaded. When Christ appears, it is usually in the context of Old Testament iconography, where he features both as part of the pantheon of great Jewish leaders and as brother to the Jews of twentieth century eastern Europe. This is particularly the case in works such as *The Creation of Man* and *The Sacrifice of Isaac*, part of the series of monumental canvases produced in the 1950s and 60s known as the Biblical Message cycle (housed mostly in the Museum of the Biblical Message Marc Chagall in Nice); but it is also true of the stained glass windows and work in other media he produced for the Christian Church. That he initially had some misgivings about working for the latter is confirmed by the fact that in 1950 he sought the blessing of the Chief Rabbi of France and the President of Israel, before embarking on a commission for the church of Notre Dame de Toute Grâce at Assy. Significantly, the ceramic mural he eventually produced, of *Moses leading the Jews across the Red Sea* (which includes a small Christ figure in the top right hand corner) is inscribed with the words "In the name of the freedom of all religions".

Yet in the context of the Biblical Message paintings – and even more when the motif appears in one of Chagall's works for a Christian church such as Tudeley or cathedrals such as Metz, Reims and Chichester, it is difficult not to interpret the inclusion of the crucified Christ in traditional typological terms. Here, in other words, Christ easily becomes the Second Adam, come to redeem the sins of the first. Although there is plenty of evidence to prove that Chagall had no such reading of his imagery in mind, the interpretation remains a persuasive one and one that suggests a certain naïveté on the part of the artist, and a curious insensitivity to the importance of context. Naïve or not the trans-denominational popularity of Chagall's religious images suggests that his universalist and life-affirming vision of love, hope and brotherhood strikes a chord in many.

A MODERNIST MONUMENT IN RURAL KENT: CHAGALL'S STAINED GLASS WINDOWS IN ALL SAINTS' CHURCH

BY ROSALIND P. BLAKESLEY

ROSALIND P. BLAKESLEY IS SENIOR LECTURER IN THE HISTORY OF ART AND A FELLOW OF PEMBROKE COLLEGE, UNIVERSITY OF CAMBRIDGE. HER RESEARCH INTERESTS INCLUDE RUSSIAN ART AND THE ARTS AND CRAFTS MOVEMENT. HER PUBLICATIONS INCLUDE *AN IMPERIAL COLLECTION: WOMEN ARTISTS FROM THE STATE HERMITAGE MUSEUM* AND *THE ARTS AND CRAFTS MOVEMENT*.

In 1961, Lady d'Avigdor Goldsmid accompanied her elder daughter, Sarah, on a visit to Paris. While there, both mother and daughter were impressed by Marc Chagall's stained glass windows for the synagogue of the Hadassah Medical Centre in Jerusalem, which were on display in a purpose-built pavilion in the grounds of the Louvre. Their shared experience was to acquire great poignancy when Sarah died two years later in a boating accident off the coast of Rye in East Sussex. Just twenty-one years old, she and a friend drowned after spending the night astride the hull of their upturned yacht, while a third companion survived by swimming to the shore. Four years later, in 1967, Lady d'Avigdor Goldsmid and her husband, Sir Henry, resolved to commemorate Sarah's life by commissioning Chagall to design a memorial east window for a twelfth-century church near the family estate of Somerhill, Tonbridge. By 1985, all twelve of the church's windows had been replaced, making All Saints' Church in Tudeley, Kent, the site of Chagall's first stained glass commission in England, and the only church in the world to boast a complete set of windows by the Jewish artist.

Chagall's interest in ecclesiastical stained glass dated from 1950, when he expressed the desire to design a set of windows for a small, unused chapel in Vence, southern France, where he was living at the time. His first realised designs were for the church of Notre-Dame de Toute Grâce in Assy in 1957, and with the unveiling of his windows for the Hadassah Medical Centre in 1961 he had established himself as a major new practitioner in the genre. By then an artist of international renown, Chagall was initially reluctant to accept a commission for a small rural church in Kent. Sir Henry later recalled that it took his wife's greatest powers of persuasion to bring the artist round to the idea. Once he had agreed to the work, however, Chagall produced a window of remarkable intensity in which Sarah is depicted prone in the water; rising above the waves with outstretched arms; and ascending a ladder towards Christ on the cross. The tragic manner of Sarah's death is thus interwoven with a spiritual narrative befitting the east window of a working church. Chagall was thrilled with the result, exclaiming at the window's dedication in 1967: 'C'est magnifique, je ferai les tous.'

Delighted by the artist's enthusiasm, Lady d'Avigdor Goldsmid commissioned him to replace the remaining eleven windows, though the project was far from straight-forward. While seven semi-abstract windows were installed in the nave in 1974, the four chancel windows were kept in storage for a further eleven years, as some of the church's parishioners objected to the removal of the existing Victorian windows which had been designed by Mabel Emma Boscowen. (A compromise was eventually reached, whereby the Victorian windows were rehoused in light boxes in the vestry.) Nor was Chagall forthcoming with his designs. As Lady d'Avigdor Goldsmid commented in 1978: 'I am taking them absolutely on trust. We couldn't get Chagall to do a drawing – the usual procedure would be to give a drawing to the PCC {the parochial church council} and the diocesan council before the windows were made. They have the right to refuse them but I hope and pray they will not! ... I want everyone to be happy about it.' It was not until 1985, after the death of both Sir Henry and Chagall (who died at the age of ninety seven that same year), that the four chancel windows were finally installed.

For inspiration, Chagall was drawn to schemes as diverse as the medieval work at Chartres cathedral, and the stained glass windows which Matisse designed for the Notre-Dame du Rosaire chapel at Vence. At the same time, in collaboration with the stained glass craftsmen Charles and Brigitte Marq at the Atelier Jacques Simon at Reims, he developed a working method entirely his own. Charles Marq would begin by producing suitably coloured glass and then treating this with acid to achieve Chagall's subtle tonal variations. Chagall then drew and painted on the glass, applying colour washes to bring out the highlights and shadows, and adding details by scratching, rubbing, or incising with the end of a paintbrush (there are even thumb and fingerprints on parts of the Tudeley work). The Marqs played an active role throughout, visiting the site to familiarise themselves with the peculiarities of the lighting at All Saints', and rising to the challenge of meeting Chagall's highly specific colour requirements, and of translating his gouache designs into glass.

With his painterly approach and use of lead lines, which often bear no relation to the actual design, Chagall provoked the ire of stained glass purists for disregarding the innate properties of the medium. Yet his designs - emotive, vibrant, punctuated by accents of bright colour, and populated by an array of birds and beasts (not to mention a possible self-portrait in a window of the north nave) - bear witness to the extraordinary creativity of the artist even in his ninth decade. Chagall's other stained glass commissions may have received more critical attention. His windows for the cathedrals of Chichester, Metz and Reims, the Art Institute of Chicago, and the United Nations Building in New York certainly enjoy a higher public profile. Tucked away among the fields and oast houses of Kent, All Saints' Church in Tudeley nonetheless remains one of the most stunning and intimate monuments of Modernist stained glass.

Lady d'Avigdor-Goldsmid
ALL SAINT'S CHURCH
TUDELEY

TUDELEY
echelle 1/5
est

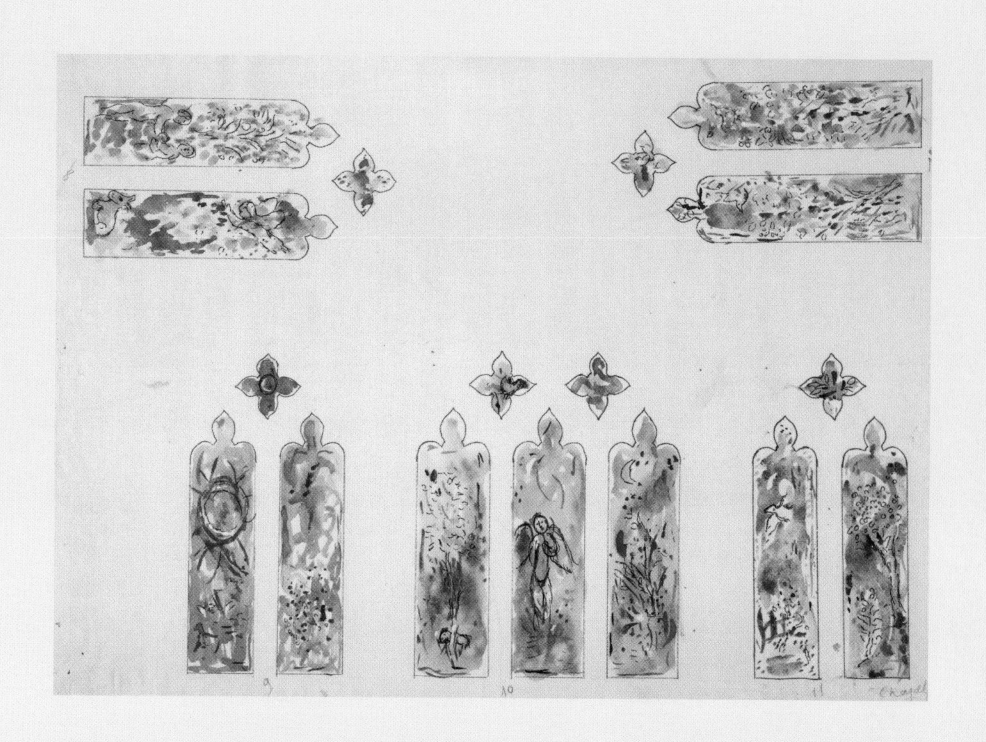

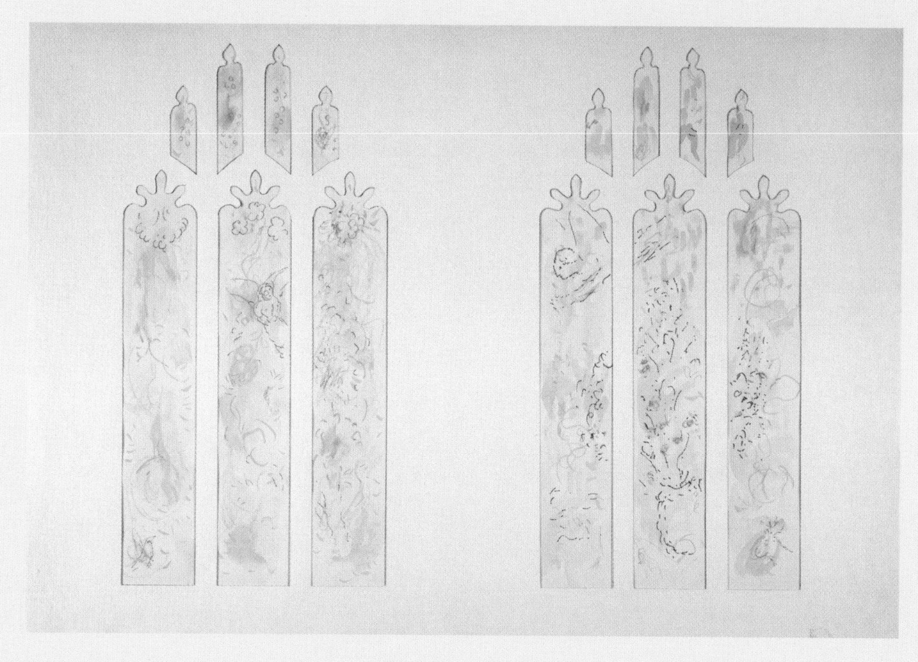

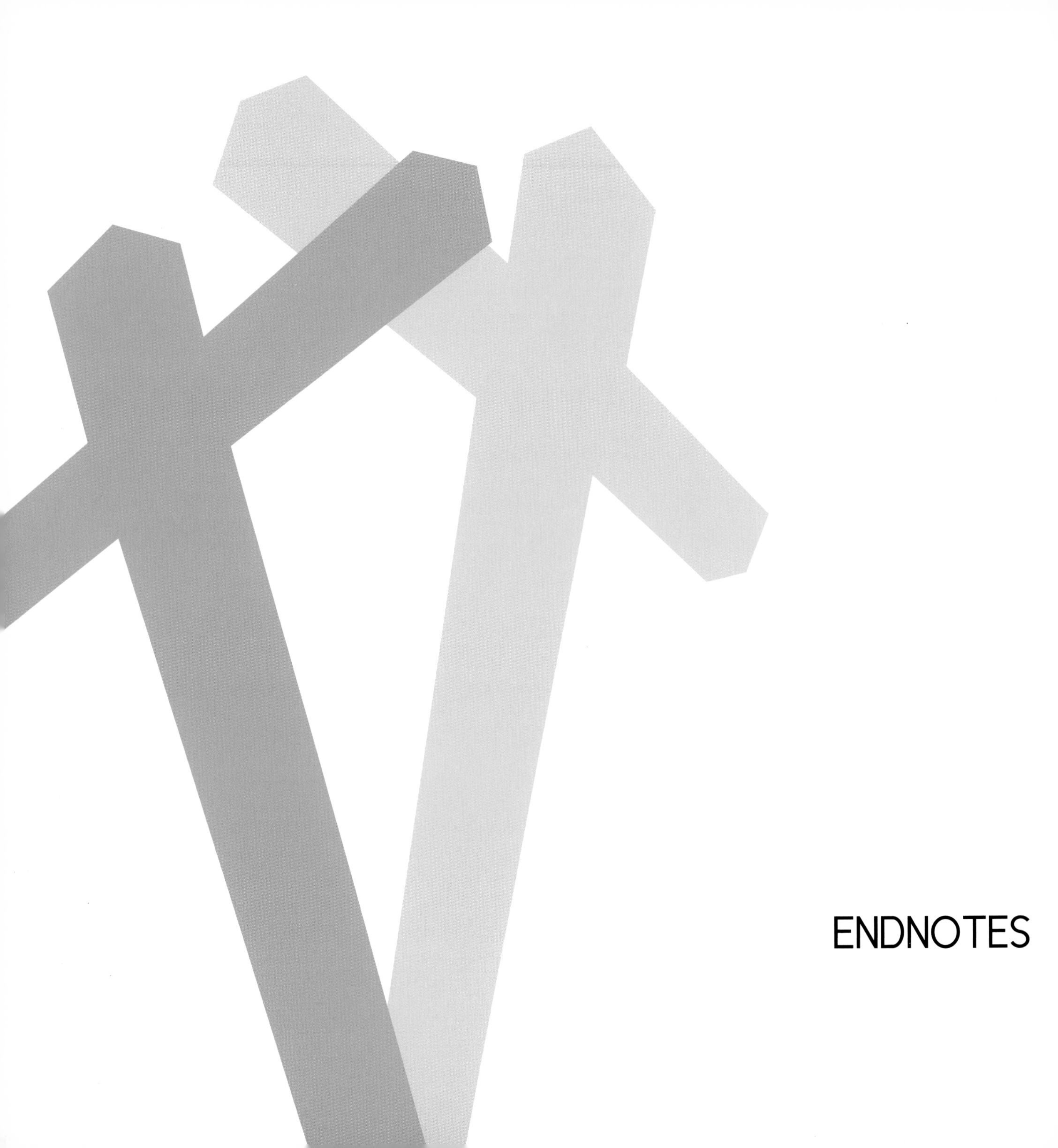

ENDNOTES

OUR VISION FOR MASCALLS GALLERY

VANESSA EVERETT, HEADTEACHER, MASCALLS SCHOOL 1999 – 2009

Mascalls Gallery was set up in 2006 as a response to the requirement for the school, as a specialist school for the visual arts, to engage with the local community. The principal aim of the gallery was to break down the barriers that prevent a large number of people in the Paddock Wood area from accessing art, and particularly modern art. We wanted to do this by running a professionally curated gallery that had access to major works from national collections as well as exhibiting emerging artists who produced work during a residency at the school – a place that students and parents are familiar with. Secondary aims were to broaden our students' horizons by introducing them to art from other cultures and also to enrich the school curriculum and improve oracy by encouraging students to develop an oral response to works of art. Since its inception, the gallery has been meeting these aims but has also meeting some that were not envisaged at the outset. These include the extensive outreach programme which enhances the education of young people all the way from reception class to Masters level and also the involvement of individuals in the community who are past retirement age and for whom the gallery offers a means of viewing world class art which they would otherwise have to travel to London to see. Over the last year the quality of the gallery's programme has attracted national attention and 2010 will mark a further development, international collaboration, with the Cross Purposes exhibition. Our great good fortune has been the creativity and drive of its curator, Nathanial Hepburn.

To me the gallery's very existence symbolises the role of education in opening up new and high quality experiences that help form the thinking of young people. In this respect, all the exhibitions have played a part but my personal highlights have been our opening exhibition of Latin American art, a remarkable exhibition by contemporary Gypsy Traveller artists which forged links with our local Traveller community and then our highly successful exhibitions of work by Lee Miller and Graham Sutherland as well as the recent, beautifully presented sculptures by Ana Maria Pacheco.

MASCALLS GALLERY – PAST EXHIBITIONS

Fumiko Ichida: Shadowmakers (12.06.06 – 24.06.06)

Stephen Bollard: Remnants of Place (03.07.06 – 28.07.06)

Subverted Icon; Pop in Latin America (01.09.06 – 14.10.06)
featuring Raul Martinez, Nadin Ospina & Cildo Meireles

Contemporary Gypsy; art & archive (06.11.06 – 09.12.09)
Delaine le Bas & Daniel Baker with archive material

Walker Evans; photographs from 1935 – 1936 (12.01.07 – 10.02.07)

This is Tomorrow; art & design 1956 & 1957 (05.03.07 – 14.04.07)

ko-ax 07 (23.04.07 – 05.05.07)

Anytown; artists' responses to the urban environment (11.06.07 – 19.07.07)
including LS Lowry, Nathan Coley, Rachel Whiteread, Freddie Robins

Contemporary Gypsy; a new visual archive (03.08.07 – 13.09.07)
local Traveller families document their lives

Andy Goldsworthy (27.10.07 – 01.12.07)

Kino Plakat: Czech film posters from the 60s and 70s (14.01.08 – 23.02.08)
from the University of Brighton Design Archives – curated by Susanne Sklepek

ko-ax 08 (08.03.08 – 05.04.08)

Henry Moore; drawings, prints & maquettes (21.04.08 – 31.05.08)

Adam Hahn; Portraits of Macular Degeneration (13.06.08 – 17.07.08)

Tom Eckersley: Poster Design (13.09.08 – 18.10.08)

Lee Miller: Portraits (03.11.08 – 13.12.08)

Graham Sutherland (12.01.09 – 21.02.09)

ko-ax 09 (06.03.09 – 04.04.09)

Telling Tales; Paintings and Sculpture from East Africa (20.04.09 – 23.05.09)

Anna Cocciadiferro; Coralline Swan Song (01.06.09 – 27.06.09)

Taking Art for a Walk (04.09.09 – 17.10.09)
Richard Long, Dominic Pote, Hamish Fulton & Scarlett Hooft Graafland – curated by and featuring Aaron Tebano

Ana Maria Pacheco 02.11.09 – 19.12.09

Edge of Abstraction 09.01.09 – 13.02.09
Bryan Wynter, Peter Lanyon, John Piper, William Scott, Alfred Wallis, Wilhelmina Barns-Graham

BEN URI - SHORT HISTORY AND MISSION STATEMENT

THE ART MUSEUM FOR EVERYONE

Founded 1st July 1915 by the Russian émigré artist Lazar Berson at Gradel's Restaurant, Whitechapel in the East End of London as 'The Jewish National Decorative Art Association (London), "Ben Ouri". The name echoed that of legendary biblical craftsman Bezalel Ben Uri, the creator of the tabernacle in the Temple of Jerusalem. It also reflects a kinship with the ideals of the famous Bezalel School of Arts and Crafts founded in Jerusalem ten years earlier in 1905.

Ben Uri Gallery is Europe's only dedicated Jewish Museum of Art working in partnership with secular and Jewish Museums in the UK and internationally. The gallery and museum is an educational institution dedicated to enhancing the quality of life of all whom it impacts. It embraces a new broad and fully inclusive role for museums in today's society and addresses contemporary issues through art and its social history. By fostering easy access, greater appreciation and both social and academic enjoyment of the visual arts, there is an ongoing opportunity to demonstrate its value as a robust and unique bridge between the cultural, religious, political differences and beliefs of our fellow citizens.

Its purpose is to enable the largest possible audience, drawn from the widest possible communities from both home and abroad, to explore for inspiration, learning and enjoyment, the work, lives and contribution of British and European artists of Jewish descent, placed where relevant alongside their non-Jewish contemporaries, within the artistic and social context of the national cultural heritage.

Its principal route to achieving this is by enabling broad, easy and straightforward physical and virtual access through location, publication, Internet and outreach to the following:

- The Permanent Collection of over 1000 works is dominated by the work of first and second generation émigré artists: the largest of its kind in the world, accessed physically or virtually via continued exhibition, research, conservation and acquisition.

- Temporary Exhibitions: curating, touring and hosting important internationally-focused exhibitions of the widest artistic appeal that, without the museum's focus, would not be seen in the UK.
- Publications: commissioning new academic research on the artists and their historical context to accompany the museum's exhibitions.
- Library and Archive: a resource dating from the turn of the 20th century, documenting and tracing in parallel the artistic and social development of the Ben Uri and Jewish artists working or exhibiting in Britain as part of the evolving British historical landscape.
- Education & Community Learning: Adults and Students through symposia, lectures, curatorial tours, publications, library research: Children through focus related lessons, visits, after school art club, family art days, competitions; 'Children Always Free' at Ben Uri!
- Schools (local, national and special needs) through artist visits and the museum's path-finding 'Art in the Open' teaching modules using the museum's collection as part of the national curriculum.
- Artists: Monthly artist peer group programmes, Ben Uri International Jewish Artists of the Year Awards Competition, guidance and affiliation benefits.
- Care in the Community: a pioneering project of 'Art as Therapy' addressing the needs of the elderly by practising artists.
- Website: providing an on-line educational and access tool, to function as a virtual gallery and artists' reference resource for students, collectors and scholars.
- Acquire c20,000 sq ft in the heart of Central London within easy walking distance of Britain's great National Art Galleries and Museums to engage with the largest audiences from the most diverse communities from home and abroad.

BEN URI – INTERNATIONAL ADVISORY BOARD

BEN URI PATRONS – THE BERSON CIRCLE

Greta & Victor Arwas
Pauline & Daniel Auerbach
Esther & Simon Bentley
Miriam & Richard Borchard
Barry Cann
Marion & David Cohen
Sheila & Dennis Cohen Charitable Trust
Nikki & Mel Corin
Beryl & Neil Davis
Suzanne & Henry Davis
Rachel & Mike Dickson
Marion & Manfred Durst
H W Fisher and Company
Wendy Fisher
Franklin family
Sue & David Glasser
Lindy & Geoffrey Goldkorn
Madelaine & Craig Gottlieb
Averil & Irving Grose
Tresnia & Gideon Harbour
Mym and Lawrence Harding
Peter Held
Morven & Michael Heller
Joan Hurst
Sandra & John Joseph
Annely Juda Fine Art
Neil Kitchener QC
Tamar Kollek
Agnes & Edward Lee
Pamela & Michael Lester
Hannah & David Lewis
Hannah Lowy & Lord Mitchell
Alastair McEwan
Jacob Mendelson Scholarship Trust
Hugh Merrell
Robin & Edward Milstein
Diana & Allan Morgenthau
Mishcon de Reya
Susan and Leo Noe
Opera Gallery, London
Osborne Samuel Gallery, London
Susan & Martin Paisner
Shoshana & Benjamin Perl
Ingrid & Mike Posen
Simon Posen
Janice & Barry Prince
Sir Adam Ridley
Ashley Rogoff
Marilyn & Anthony Rosenfelder
Blick Rothenberg
Ann & David Susman
Esther & Romie Tager
Myra Waiman
Cathy Wills
Alma & Leslie Wolfson
Sylvie & Saul Woodrow
Della & Fred Worms
Matt Yeoman

LIST OF WORKS

Norman Adams
Golden Crucifixion
1993
Watercolour on paper
114 x 168 cm
Beaux Arts, London
p. 60

Craigie Aitchison
Crucifixion IX
1963
Oil on canvas
25 x 20 cm
Pallant House Gallery, Chichester
p. 54

Sybil Andrews
Golgotha
1931
Linoprint
30 x 20 cm
Towner Art Gallery, Eastbourne
p. 30

John Armstrong
Crucifixion
1958
Oil on canvas
82 x 112 cm
Private collection
p. 48

Samuel Bak
Study I
1995
Oil on linen
45 x 55 cm
Pucker Gallery, Boston
p. 62

Robert Henderson Blyth
In the Image of Man
1947
Oil on canvas
127 x 101.6 cm
Imperial War Museum
p. 44

Marc Chagall
Apocalypse en Lilas, Capriccio
1945
Gouache, ink and pencil on paper
51 x 36 cm
Ben Uri Gallery
p. 42

Marc Chagall
Drawings for All Saints' Church, Tudeley
1966 – 78
Mixed media on paper
Various sizes
Centre Pompidou, Paris
p. 76

Tracey Emin
The Disposition
1989
Monoprint
30 x 40 cm
Private collection
p. 58

Eric Gill
Christ Crucified
1921
Oak relief, with added colour
111.8 x 58.5 x 7.6 cm
Brighton & Hove Museums
p. 26

Duncan Grant
Drawing for Crucifixion
c.1942
Mixed media painting on paper
217 x 151 cm
Towner Art Gallery, Eastbourne
p. 36

Maggi Hambling
Good Friday
2002
Oil on canvas
56 x 46 cm
Courtesy of the artist
p. 64

David Jones
Sanctus Christus de Capel-y-ffin
1925
Gouache and pencil on paper
19 x 13 cm
Tate
p. 28

Emmanuel Levy
Crucifixion
1942
Oil on Canvas
102 x 78 cm
Ben Uri Gallery
p. 34

Roy de Maistre
Crucifixion
1942–44
Oil
130 x 92 cm
Leicester Museums
p. 38

Lee Miller
Hotline to God
1944
Photograph
Lee Miller Archives, England
p. 40

Michael Rothenstein
The Crucifixion
1937
Oil on board
101.6 x 76.2 cm
Tate
p. 32

Francis Newton Souza
Crucifixion
1959
Oil on board
195 x 134 cm
Tate
p. 52

Gilbert Spencer
The Crucifixion
1915
Oil on canvas
104.5 x 116.4 cm
Tate
p. 24

Stanley Spencer
Drawings for the Crucifixion
1958
Pencil on paper
Aldenham School
p. 50

Graham Sutherland
Crucifixion
1947
Oil on Board
65 x 40 cm
Pallant House Gallery, Chichester
p. 46

Betty Swanwick
The Lost Wilderness
1974–75
Pencil
50 x 38 cm
Private Collection
p. 56

ACKNOWLEDGEMENTS

Aldenham School: Andrew Fraser | Beaux Arts London: Reg, Patricia and Louis Singh | Ben Uri: Suzanne Lewis, David Glasser | Brighton Museum & Art Gallery: Jenny Lund, Stella Beddoe | Centre Pompidou, Paris | Chris Beetles Gallery | IAP Fine Art: David Tregunna | Imperial War Museum: Ulrike Smalley | Lee Miller Archives: Anthony Penrose, Ami Bouhassane | Leicester Museum & Galleries: Simon Lake | Maggi Hambling | Pallant House Gallery, Chichester: Simon Martin, Stefan van Raay | Pucker Gallery, Boston: Bernie & Sue Pucker | Tate: Nicole Simoes da Silva, Robert Upstone, Chris Stephens, Matthew Gale | Timothy Taylor: Juliet Bailey, Terry Danziger-Miles | Towner, Eastbourne: Sara Cooper, Matthew Rowe

Design by: Helen Robertson, www.helenrobertson.com

Typeface: Cicle, designed by Joan Alegret

Printers: Tadberry Evedale Ltd.

mascallsgallery

The Art Museum for Everyone
The London Jewish Museum of Art, Bridging Communities since 1915